Bare Feet, Chicken Beaks, and Blackberry Pie

Kristi J. Shingley
Romans 1:16

BARE FEET, CHICKEN BEAKS AND BLACKBERRY PIE

Marti J. Powell Shrigley

XULON PRESS

Xulon Press
2301 Lucien Way #415
Maitland, FL 32751
407.339.4217
www.xulonpress.com

Unless otherwise indicated, Scripture quotations taken from the King James Version (KJV)–*public domain.*

Printed in the United States of America.

ISBN-13: 978-1-54564-514-7

Dedication

This book is dedicated to my prince of a husband, Larry, who not only walked this journey with me, but lived it as well. I love you, Darling. Never could I have had a better mate.

In loving memory of Mark Mandelstein

Mark was one of the men mentioned in this book who accepted Christ a few short months ago. A great friend of mine. Fifty-nine years old and seemingly in good health. His death was totally unexpected and a shock to those of us who loved him. The timing of his death, just as I'd finished writing this, is proof positive that time, truly, is of the essence. Our next breath is not promised. It could be at the next blink of our eyes that our soul will be demanded.

Mark, you will be sorely missed, but I will see you again. Until that day, keep the soup warm and the coffee hot!

Psalm 92:14,
"They shall still bring forth fruit in old age;
they shall be fat and flourishing."

Heartfelt thanks and acknowledgements

A few girls, with whom I graduated, get together once a month for lunch. I was reminded that I was the one complaining that I had nothing to do. Life was boring—and then I got cancer. Things changed, all for the good! I can hardly contain my enthusiasm when I'm around them. I blather on and on—so, thanks, gals, for putting up with me. I love you all!

To Phyllis and Wanda, without you, this story would not have been. Three, we stand! Love you.

And, again, to my sisters, and my cousin Sheila, for listening on the days that were a little gray for me. You were the light that brightened my days. And for your prayers...your precious prayers. Thanks! I love you dearly!

There are many, many friends that I would like to thank for their prayers and encouragement. You know who you are! Those of you who took the time to write and to pray. Thank you. You got me through chemo and kept me strong.

The guys and gals at the Cancer Center who poked all that poison into me that I might live! You tried to save my life as I tried to save your soul. And to my precious doctors, for your wisdom and compassion. Thank you.

To my husband, my children, their spouses, grandchildren, and Brian, all who were only a text away...only God knows how much I love you. Thank you from the depth of my soul for being there for me. I love you all so much!

Especially, a great big thanks to Mommy and Daddy. There are no words. I love you and will see you soon!

And last but not least, I want to acknowledge my bestie, Joyce, my little prayer warrior, who rallied the troops on my behalf. Always there for me. Thanks for nagging me to finish what I start. I would that each of you should have a friend such as she! Hey, Joycie! Maybe our mansions WILL be next to each other!

Just a fun little story...I always laugh when I think of this.

A few years ago, Lar and I flew to Oregon for our yearly getaway. I always get a little nauseated on planes, so I brought a large bottle of "Tums for the tummy" to make the trip a little more comfortable for me. Well, to make a long story short, by the time we arrived in Portland, I had chewed and swallowed half the bottle of pills. I must have thought they were going to help with my nerves, too.

We picked up our rental and started down the coast. All seemed well—for a while. Then my stomach started to gurgle. Didn't think much about it. We spotted this neat little shop and stopped to browse. I hadn't been on my feet for more than five minutes when gas bubbles started to form. One bubble after another lined up in my intestinal walls...until combustion took place. I mean—every few steps that I took—I dropped one. *Atomic proportion.* Lethal, for sure. I single-handedly funked up every aisle in that small store. I was honestly just trying to get out of there, but I couldn't move very fast. All around, people were dropping like fumigated flies. I didn't dare look back at the carnage.

I stumbled out of the shop, gasping for air, followed by the herd of coughing and choking people. Needless to say, it was a miserable night for me, but for Lar, it was intolerable. He was so mad at me, I thought our marriage was over. But, by the next morning, things were nearly back to normal. All except for an occasional "pop" here and there.

I learned a very valuable lesson from that experience. Don't ever take forty Tums at one time, especially if you don't want to be charged with murder. I also learned that you don't have to be dead to smell like it!

Table of Contents

Foreword

The most widely read book in history is the Bible. It contains a variety of writing styles; one of my favorites is parables. Parables are earthly stories with heavenly meaning. In Marti's light-hearted book, she shares her life experiences through which nuggets of wisdom are revealed . If you are struggling to find the "why" behind your life's difficult journey; Marti's modern-day parables are sure to help you along the way.

Pastor John Hays, Jersey Church

Preface

As I was sorting through a kitchen drawer a few days ago, I came upon an old pair of binoculars. They'd been made back when things had some quality to them. They were heavy, black metal with thick, perfectly-clear lenses. I ran my fingers over the long bumpy cylinders and then put them up to my eyes. Through the small end, everything seemed large and close, but when I reversed them and peered through the large end, things were very, very small and very, very distant. It was as though I was viewing my life in the past and my life in the future. My past life was so far in the distance, but I could still see it. I stared long and hard at the objects around me, taking in as much detail as I could. As I peered through the lenses, visions of my childhood started to bubble up into the forefront of my memory banks. I saw myself as a small child. I saw my sisters, my mom and dad, my pets, and people that had once been young and vibrant, all part of my life. Teachers, preachers, classmates, loved ones of old.

Memories, no matter how large or small, by themselves seem insignificant. But when collected and placed into a mental collage, they manifest into an intricate picture of what we call *life*. The bright memories are shades of red, orange, and yellow. The tender ones—blues, pinks, and greens. Black and gray are the shadows and down times of our lives. Arranged and pieced together until they join, they produce a masterpiece...an Aurora Borealis across the span of time.

Choosing to capitalize on the good memories and minimizing the rest has helped me to appreciate life to its fullest.

It's funny how we grow through the years and yet don't notice it happening until we looked backwards. The days, months, and years pass, and yet it is like a puff of wind that blows past our ears. As we age, I think that it must be normal that we occasionally take stock of what we have accomplished by glancing over our shoulders. In an instant, I've gone from young to old without a stop in the intermediate. I find myself standing near the end of the road and I'm not sure how I got here.

Nevertheless, here I am, and I am taking stock.

Smack Dab in the Middle

I guess one could say that my life, thus far, can be summed up with one word—mediocrity. Born the middle child of three sisters in the middle of the century to middle-class parents. Not overweight, not underweight for sure, not multi-talented, but not without talent. Intelligent, but not overly so. I felt more *safe* than *loved*, but not by that much. Right in the middle. Yeah, this has been my life.

It has taken me many years to accept being mediocre, but because of it, I am well-adjusted and balanced. Being the middle sister of three has not always been easy, but I rather like being in the middle. Not too much pressure! I can look at myself and laugh. Really laugh! "Ain't life grand?"

I was not very observant as a child. I went my own way, did my own thing within the confines of my parents' rules, which were not too strict, but definitely strict enough. I had self-worth, but surely knew that I was not indispensable.

I am a baby boomer, if you please, born after Dad returned from the war. Born at a time when so many other "boomers" came into the world. I didn't even have a birthday of my own. I was my five-year-old sister's birthday present. Never had a cake of my own without multiple candles representing our combined years. Mom always liked Phyllis best, but I handled it and enjoyed my junior position for two years until our baby sister, Wanda, was born. Phyllis and I were both pushed aside to accommodate the cute, curly-headed, smart little cherub that now sat on the top of the totem pole of adoration. In fact, instead of sharing a bedroom with me and allowing Phyllis her own, Wanda had her own room which she shared with all of her imaginary friends. But that's the way it was. *Spoiled* rights apparently went to the baby just as *bossiness* rights went to the eldest.

Stuck in the middle again, or so I thought, but it wasn't long before I realized that as far as the totem pole goes, I didn't even come close to the center. I was as low as I could get, a rank that was established very early in my life.

Kid Sisters—Yikes!

B aby Wanda always got her way from the get-go.
Not only was my little sister the apple of Mom's
eye, but also of my older sister's. I may have been
Phyllis' birthday gift, but I was not her baby doll.
She hovered over that little kid like a mother hen
over her chicks. I thought that Wanda was a strange
little child. She spent her days playing tea party
with her teddies and dollies. When I'd sneak up to
her bedroom door and push it open, just enough
for me to spy in on her and her socialite friends, it
was like beholding a Broadway production in full
bloom. Props, costumes, and all the set decorations.

Imaginary play would come to a halt when I
could no longer stand the solace and peace that
she was so intensely enjoying. I would interrupt
her trance-like state by stealing one of her guests
as they sat around the tea table. If I were lucky, I
would cash in on a crumpet or two. I'd run through
the house, dragging along a doll, held by her hair,
with a teddy bear tucked under my arm. My kid
sister screamed at the top of her lungs over the
abduction of her loved ones. It was quite a familiar
scene, repeated often in the household.

And, of course, Wanda would run to Mom or
to Phyllis—whoever was the handiest—and as I

positively knew, I would be in hot water. It wasn't that I was a slow learner. I just couldn't resist making her miserable. Maybe it was the fact that I'd never cared for dolls or silly playtime and I was jealous of anyone who had a creative mind. If I couldn't see it, I couldn't imagine it. Therefore, most of my play was out-of-doors, where there were trees to climb, chickens to chase, kittens to kiss and hug.

Pre-School

P reschool memories have all but vanished, but surface from time to time with certain sights, smells, or sounds. Each fall, the sound of locusts chirping, heralding in Autumn with all its glorious colors and beauty, transports me back to my early years before school days.

I stood in the front yard of my grandparents' farm home, frozen by fear, from the unfamiliar raspy voices of cicadas. Looking up through the leaves of the gigantic maple tree, I could see hundreds of bright red eyes staring back at me. Had anyone ever taken the time to explain to me that every late summer, our countryside would be overtaken by thousands and thousands of these creatures? No. On the farm, you found out things by happenstance. And sooner or later, you put two and two together and realized that this happens every year before the weather turns cold. They are harbingers of things to come.

For whatever reason, there is always an excitement when I hear their song. Perhaps the thought of snow, holidays, or warm cuddly nights in front of the fireplace. But more than likely it is the thought of big fat popcorn balls and warm cocoa with tons of marshmallows. This says winter to me!

Painted Ladies

Phyllis babysat for Wanda and me on more than one occasion while Mom helped the men in the hay field. She usually did a pretty good job of keeping us safe, especially since I was a curious three-year-old and Wanda, a babe in diapers. Occasionally, she was asked to multitask, which she usually handled quite well.

One day, not only was she chief-bottle washer and diaper changer, but Mom also gave her the chore of painting a little handmade stool that our uncle had crafted for her. What fun! She had never painted before, and I guess in the excitement of it all, Wanda and I got misplaced somewhere in Phyllis' mind.

She sorted through the many cans of leftover paint that Grandad had stacked in the shed until she found the perfect color for her stool. Maroon! Very, very bright maroon. Brush in hand, can in the other, she warned us to get out of her way, so that she could start her important furniture-painting chore.

Dunk, slap, brush. Dunk, slap, brush. Her hands moved back and forth over the little seat and her pride swelled with each stroke. Her face shined as much as the new, glossy paint on the stool.

At first, it was kind of fun watching her gussy up her new possession, but to a three-year-old, she might as well have been painting a barn! I soon grew tired of the repetition of dunk, slap, brush and moved on to more exciting things. Wheels started to roll as I spied an extra paint brush lying beside the paint can.

She dunked and turned her back to me. My time was not wasted. I grabbed the brush and did a little dunking of my own. The first dip into the can went up to my elbow. Upon pulling it out, I realized I had nothing to paint. My eyes quickly scoped the surrounding area, when they landed on the only object with painting potential—Wanda.

I dismissed the idea of painting her, until I looked down my arm and saw my beautiful maroon-mahogany colored skin.

Once again, my eyes focused on Wanda. Although, I knew better, I couldn't resist the temptation of having a beautiful little Indian baby as a sister. Phyllis was mesmerized by her own painting ability and was oblivious to what went on behind her. Quickly, I performed my task of changing Wanda from Caucasian to Indian. I stood back, took a good look at her, and gasped with astonishment at my talent. The transformation was remarkable. So remarkable, I decided to change my race also! I had to really work quickly now. Phyllis was putting on the finishing touches. With her last stroke, she stood back to admire her handiwork. Beaming with pride, she took one more step backward and bumped into Wanda—which snapped her out of her trance. Oh, yes, that's right, she was supposed to be babysitting! She reached her hand around behind her. Realizing that her hand must have had paint on it, she whirled around to see how much paint she had gotten on Wanda.

With one glance, the blood drained from her face, clear to her feet. She was as white as we were red. No sooner had she spotted Wanda, in a blink she caught me out of the corner of her eye. Panic was written all over her face. Panic turned to sheer terror in the same instant she heard Mom heading down the hill on Nellie Belle, our old Massey Ferguson tractor. You could hear Mom singing over the roar of the motor until she hit the driveway and spotted her once-beautiful brown-haired previously-white girls, now painted from head to toe in the most hideous mess of purplish red-brown oil paint.

No sooner had her feet hit terra firma, when all three of us were whisked down to the gasoline pump, where we encountered the most vigorous scrubbing of our young lives. The fumes nearly suffocated us, not to mention the blistering of tender skin. She meant business. I'm lucky to be alive to tell this, but sad to say, this was only the first of the many times that Mom tried to kill us!

School Days

Even though precious little is etched into my mind of my school years, I do seem to have some very vivid memory-pictures of my early grade-school experiences. Some, I remember with fondness and joy. There are a few circumstances that I would rather forget, but for the most part, the good times overshadowed the bad.

As with most children, my two favorite times during the school day were lunch and recess. Our two lunch-ladies faithfully prepared delicious hot meals for us each day. Not the heat-and-eat kind of food that you get at school these days. Lunch was from-scratch, home-cooked meals. Real mashed potatoes, hot pork sandwiches, fresh vegetables, homemade bread...and desserts to die for. I, for one, was always grateful for those delicious feasts cooked and served by our lunch-ladies.

We scarfed down our meals as quickly as we could, so we could get to the playground where we could be...*ourselves*. We spent our time hitting each other, calling names, tattling, and ripping each other's clothes off, so that we could be the first in line to play whatever game it was that we were playing that day. It must have looked rather strange to see one kid gouging out another's eye while asking,

"Mother, may I?" No one ever had the patience to wait his turn.

Our playground equipment was pretty much standard for the time. We had swings, slides, and monkey bars—where the word "modesty" was never mentioned. Girls would hang upside down, for hours at a time. Our dresses dangled over our heads, but no one seemed to notice. Sashes (usually held in place only by a thin loop of thread) were ripped from dress waistbands. Skirts were torn. Pockets and the seats of boys' pants were ripped on the metal slide. Lifetime neck and spinal injuries were sustained from repeated jumps, falls, and accidentally-on-purpose pushes from the swings.

But the piece of equipment that was loved and feared by all was the "ocean wave." It made its appearance in my second or third year of school. I'm sure that the inventor of this nifty piece of entertainment never had children of his own, at least none that he apparently loved. Used in a supervised and controlled manner, the ocean wave could lull one to sleep with its gentle back and forth, around and around motion. But with one turn of the teacher's head, every kid's foot hit the ground, running and pushing as fast as humanly possible. Around and around, faster and faster it would go until bodies were catapulted into the next county.

Blood-curdling screams, and sounds of flesh hitting metal, other bodies, or the dirt would draw the supervisor's attention back to her charges. A mass of bleeding children was usually found lying under or around the behemoth.

It was standard procedure for the teacher to send one of the older students out after recess, basket in hand, to pick up various pieces of clothing, body parts, and the remains of smaller children that were scattered in the vicinity of "the wave." No matter the number of casualties, we couldn't wait until the bell rang for the next recess. A triage became a permanent fixture in the foyer of the school. By the time school started the next fall, we were minus our most treasured activity. Seems there may have been too many severed fingers and concussions! Go figure!

No playground would have existed back in the fifties without outside restrooms. The "privy" was our refuge, fortress, shelter, and meeting place. Many a time, my life was spared because of the "girls only" sign. Most of the girls ran to the safety of the toilet when being chased by a boy who was threatening to kiss her. Not in my case. If I were ever chased to the toilet by a boy, it was because he wanted to beat the tar out of me for some reason or the other.

Love letters were read in the secrecy of this little building. Girl talks and good cries were experienced there. My first real gift from a boy was opened in the privacy of the outhouse, in the presence of a dozen or so friends, all wrapped in white tissue paper bedecked with a bouquet of purple violets. Kind of warms your heart, doesn't it?

Scarcely a day went by, especially in the winter, that our poor old janitor was not summoned to retrieve something that had fallen into the latrine. A glove, mitten, button, homework...you name it. How he ever managed to squeeze through those tiny, kid-sized toilet holes still baffles me!

On the school playground, even a simple game such as jump rope turned into a battle of the sexes. Boys against girls and vice-versa. Each time the girls had a jump rope game in progress, some nasty boy came along and grabbed the rope and ran like the wind, leaving the girl in the middle still jumping up and down, oblivious to the dirty deed which had been committed.

Time after time this happened, until one day I reckoned in my heart that we girls would not stand for this abuse any longer. Surely enough, the final jump rope championship was being held and here came the enemy, sneering and jeering all the way. I was one of the *turners*. The closer he came, the tighter I clenched the rope. Then it happened. He grabbed the rope and off he ran. Only this time, I was still attached to the other end! All was well... for a second. Then I realized that this kid was an Olympic runner and I was not! I was being dragged in the dirt like a tail on a kite, ready for lift-off. On and on he ran, leaving a trail of my skin and blood on the ground, with his every footstep. I coughed as

I swallowed dust, dirt, gravel, and bugs. It seemed like an eternity.

Finally, the bell rang.—When I came to, I stared at my hands in utter amazement. They were still attached to my arms and the rope was still clenched in my fists! Victory was ours! We had won the war! I was bruised from my hips to my knees, but it was a small price to pay for victory. Jumping rope was out of the question for me for a few weeks, but all was worth it. He never bothered us again, but, somehow jump rope was never quite the same.

For the sake of nostalgia, I went back there a few months ago. The schoolhouse and playground are no longer. And in their stead are underbrush and large trees. Pieces of stained glass from the old church, which stood adjacent to the beloved site, can still be seen if the sunlight hits them just right.

I stood quietly, and for a second—a very brief second, I could hear children laughing and playing. I heard the chains on the swings squeaking and the recess bell signaling that the fun was over and time for study was at hand. I could see my first-grade teacher tucking a handkerchief neatly into the wrist of her right sleeve after wiping the eyes of some small child and then blowing the nose of another with the same hanky. There was much comfort in that soggy handkerchief and those gentle hands that offered it to us. No Kleenex could ever take its place.

Nashport Elementary 5ᵗʰ grade class. Top row, third from left.

Am I My Sister's Keeper?

Kid sisters can be so annoying! Most times I was proud of my baby sister and was very protective of her, but there were times that she embarrassed me to death.

Once a year, our school had "little sister or brother day" and we were encouraged to bring one of our small siblings to school with us for a few hours. Kind of like bringing your pet to school for show-and-tell. A couple days before this, I spent my time planning what Wanda would wear, the bow and "do," shoes and socks, coat, right down to her underwear. Good thing! I no sooner got her off the school bus and settled into the classroom, when she had to use the bathroom.

Not wanting to be embarrassed by taking my kid sister to the outside toilet, I ignored Mom's *three million warnings* "not to let that kid out of your sight for one minute." I aimed my three-year-old sister in the direction of the latrine and pointed to the little brown building with the word "Girls" marked on it. Who cared that she couldn't read? I watched her short, little legs as she made it down the concrete steps, then headed off across the play yard. I went back to my room, took my seat, and promptly forgot all about her.

Some ten to fifteen minutes later, the principal came to our room and asked to speak with me. I noticed a grin on his face and, with barely-contained humor, he informed me that my little sister was outside, calling for me.

I thought that I'd felt embarrassment from forgetting about her...until I walked out of the school building and saw her running back and forth across the yard. The skirt of her dress had been scooped up in her arms, her underpants were down around her ankles, her bare butt shining in the morning sun. She had been continuously yelling at the top of her lungs, "Martha, come wipe me!" Tears were streaming down her cheeks and goo was coming out of her nose. I had to wipe both ends! Disgusting!

Phyllis, being five years my senior, pretended that she didn't know me at school, but with Wanda being two years my junior and, also puny, I felt obligated to protect her. There were only a few instances on the playground that warranted the need.

Most days, things were quiet with only a few cases of blood splattered on the playground. Occasionally, we would see the bullies beating the waddings out of each other. Groups gathered to watch the malicious goings on. One didn't dare cheer for one over the other, for fear of going home in a body bag. Once in a while, one of the older kids would step in and try to stop the fight, only to be bashed in the side of the head, then kicked to the curb. We all learned that it was best to let these things resolve themselves.

There was one particularly nasty kid in the school who was about as big as a minute but as tough as nails. He was in Wanda's class and, for whatever reason, he thought her to be an easy target. One day, as I was skidding down the slide, I noticed a crowd forming around the merry-go-round. "There must be fight," I thought to myself. So, as soon as my feet hit the ground, I high-tailed it across the yard to watch the action. I shoved my way through the yelling and jeering spectators, only to see my kid sister being squished up against the center post of the merry-go-round. Herbie had backed up against the out-side post, put both feet on Wanda's stomach, and was pushing as hard as he could. Several of the older kids were whirling the merry-go-round as fast as they could, while others cheered from the sidelines.

It was an extremely hot and humid day and I knew that it would only take a few more whirls and a few more squishes until Wanda was not going to be around much longer. This was a dilemma and I had to make a decision. Do I step in and stop the go-round and save my sister or should I act like I don't know her and cheer with all those around me?

As they whizzed past me, I looked at Wanda's face. Her eyes bulged like that of a victim, held in the grip of a python snake. Her face was as red as wine, her mouth opened as wide as it could, but no sound emerged. Lack of oxygen, I realized. Compassion overwhelmed my survival instincts.

I lunged for the bar to stop it, when I caught a glimpse of her oppressor's eyes—wild, determined, and driven with the excitement of defeating an opponent. I retracted my steps. Although I was three times his size, I knew in his state of mind that he would bend me into a pretzel.

I stood there contemplating what to do. The recess bell rang. My decision was made. Like a rat abandoning a sinking ship, I took off for my room, leaving Wanda to fend for herself.

I don't know how much longer she was held captive or who eventually rescued her, but she was on the school bus that afternoon...looking a little green around the gills, but she had survived. Like I said, "Some things are best left to resolve themselves!"

Wanda Powell
Reserve Cheerleader

Totem pole topper!

Fire At Will!

By dinnertime that evening, Wanda was feeling well enough to eat. Of course, I always did. I cleaned my plate and ask for her leftovers. Wanda was a picky eater, so I knew that I could count on her rejects. Phyllis was not much better, so if I were lucky I might score big on a favorite meal that night. Chicken and noodles! One of Mom's specialties.

Before I got the word, "please" out of my mouth, an altercation broke out between Wanda and Phyllis. I couldn't believe it. For once, I was not involved... not yet. After some back-and-forth word slinging, Wanda loaded her fork with noodles, positioned the handle on the table, pulled back the tines, and took aim at her opponent.

As I was stuffing mashed potatoes into my mouth, my eyes flitted back and forth between the two of them. Their voices got progressively louder. My adrenaline started to surge along with the volume. Then came the threats, numerous and fast, spewing out of each mouth. Wanda ever so precisely realigned her weapon as Phyllis started to weave and bob to distract her attacker.

After what seemed to be an eternity of empty threats, I just couldn't stay out of it any longer. "Go ahead! Shoot! Go ahead, I dare you!"

Wanda squinted her eyes in my direction, turned the handle of the fork and, like a cornered cobra, let the venom fly. Strands of noodles and gravy slid down my face and onto my chest. I tried to salvage what I could. After all, they were home-made noodles.

The two enemies had become allies and were laughing at me, scorn apparent in their sneering. I crawled off my chair in shame and walked to the bathroom, picking noodles off of my shoulders and cramming them into my mouth as I went. I just never could leave well enough alone.

Charlie Brown

I wish there had been one thing in my life as a kid that I could do better than Wanda. I was jealous of everything that she did, and she was good at everything she tried. Of course, Mom bragged on her at every turn. It even came down to my being jealous of her mud pies.

Down by the garage was a heap of natural clay. It only took a little rain and the consistency was perfect for all the neat art projects that we wanted to make. My craft? Snakes, mud balls, and pies. Wanda's? Dinosaurs, elephants, tigers. All intricate, but the one that got me the most was a little *Charlie Brown* face. Each of us ran to the house, gingerly holding our handiwork out for Mom to praise. With a short glance and an insincere "nice" comment about my pie, she took one look at Wanda's "object d'art" and nearly jumped up and down with pride. After examining it carefully, she announced that she would dry it in the oven and shellac it to preserve it for all posterity. Mine? Thrown out the door! That did a lot for my self-esteem!

Day in and day out, I had to look at that stupid face (Charlie Brown's—not Wanda's). There was only so much a child could take. The jealousy on my part grew to the point of no return. The little clay face mocked me at every turn. I'm not quite sure what ever happened to old Chuck. I think my mind may have blocked it out, but I'm sure it was not a happy ending for him. I always seemed to have a way of disposing of the evidence and going on with my life. There may have been small shards of hardened clay on the back patio that were unexplained and a hammer or two that had mysteriously been moved to the wrong spot on Dad's work bench.

Who cared if no one liked my art? I had a special place that I could go and didn't have to bring my artwork home. Nearly every afternoon after school, I headed out for the big dogwood tree, which served as shade for a huge flat "writing" rock. The rock was perfect as an oversized canvas. I picked several small rocks of different colors and went to work. I spent hours there. At least I had no one to compete against except myself. In my eyes, I gave Michelangelo a run for his money. Angels, people, animals, no problem. I could draw them all. I knew what they were *supposed* to be.

I rather liked my own company. When I'd get bored with my drawings, I spent time hanging upside-down from the old apple tree behind our house. I don't know what it is that makes you imagine wonderful things when you hang upside-down, but I would love to do it again.

Super Kid

Running, jumping, and dancing were great activities that, as younger siblings, we liked to do. Phyllis, by that time was eleven or twelve years old and was into teenager-mode and would no longer get with the program.

Wanda and I took turns trying to top each other's feats. If I did cheerleading, I jumped perhaps three inches off the ground. Wanda's turn yielded cartwheels, splits, and somersaults. My cartwheels were always lop-sided and not really much of a cartwheel. It was my turn. I got a running start and tried to do *something*. I'm not sure what. That was always part of my problem. I never had a plan and certainly no commitment. No follow-through. Of course, it's hard to follow through when you don't know what you are going do in the first place. It's a vicious cycle! Well, I did my *whatever* it was. Wanda's turn.

She took her running start. "She's doing the same thing I did! What a copycat. No originality!" I scoffed.

All of a sudden and in a micro-second, she planted both feet on the ground and did a perfect no-handed flip. And she stuck it! How was this possible? Can people really do this? Well, I was done for the day. Bested again by Super Kid!

The Freezer is Not a Lollipop!

I suppose that I could have done something other than watch, in astonished horror, as blood spurted out of Wanda and life ebbed from her little body—onto the freshly-painted cement of our front porch. It was a lovely, quiet place with a swing and plenty of room to roller skate back and forth the entire width of our home. We had only one rule for the porch and that was not to touch the freezer that stood in the corner. It sat well away from *kid traffic*. Warnings abounded, don't touch any part of it. And surely not the coils. But who can blame a thirsty, hot little kid who just wanted to have one lick of the nice frosty crust of ice that formed on the coils. I used every bit of self-control not to disobey Mom's rule. But Wanda just couldn't resist the ice crystals as they glistened in the hot summer sun. Her will power crashed.

After glancing to her left and then to a right, to check for possible Mom informants, she was satisfied that the coast was clear. Wanda stuck her tongue out and quickly leaned toward a coil until there was contact.

Much to her surprise, when she moved to pull back from the freezer, her tongue didn't come with her. After a few more healthy tugs with no results, she started to panic. Wide-eyed, I ran to see what all the commotion was about, and timing being everything, I arrived at precisely the same moment that she gave the old heave-ho to release the beast's grip. A horror flick sported no more gore than the scene that I beheld.

The poor kid was obviously in pain, but fear played the major role of her emotions, and mine, too. In times past, whenever we were hurt in some way, Mom assured us that if there was no blood, everything was fine. But this time there was blood, lots of BLOOD!

The world had come to an end. Didn't matter whose blood it was, it was all over. The kid was dead. There was no hope!

I started to swoon. No one has ever been able to count on me in a crisis and, that day, I held true to form.

My body hit the deck. Phyllis came running to the scene, grabbed a cloth, stuffed it into the screaming kid's mouth, and escorted her into the house. By the time she reached Mom, Wanda was a quart low, but Mom patched her up, and after many boxes of raisins and a few bottles of Geritol, the little waif's dipstick registered "full" once again.

None of us were ever tempted to take a lick from the "ice coils of death" again. The freezer never had to be removed from its place on the porch. The popsicle temptation was forever removed with one swift jerk of the tongue. But most importantly, we all learned that Mom knew what she was talking about. If you see blood, be sure to panic. The words are synonymous!

Mom's Tight Ship

Mom ran a tight ship, be it beast or kid, house or barn. If someone or something lived in it, it had to be cleaned. She de-fleaed, de-loused, and de-bugged more kids and animals than I care to mention, and chickens were no exception. They were periodically examined and if just one louse was found, an emergency dust and fumigation campaign was launched.

Only one product would do for this project, the canister of DDT, with the dreaded skull and crossbones on it. She reasoned that this had to be good stuff to earn a prestigious label such as this. I'm sure that protective gear was suggested in the warning on the box—which to Mom, consisted of a handkerchief tied backwards on her head so as not to get the powder in her hair. She ordered each of us girls to "stand back, she was going in." Obediently, we stood back and covered our noses. At least "we" had some sense.

We watched and listened in astonishment as Mom entered the doorway of the "quarantined" building. With every chicken's squawk followed by Mom's boisterous "gotcha!" our eyes opened wider and wider. It was hard to tell who was winning the *Dust Bowl* from our view, but soon a large mushroom cloud of poison hung over and around the coop. We could hear Mom coughing and choking, but we knew that she was as plucky as any of those fowl and she would not go down in defeat.

Half an hour later, Mom emerged with a solid inch of *white death* covering every part of her body, except her hair! She grinned from ear-to-ear and proclaimed victory over every bug for as far away as the eye could see. No longer would they be a threat to her egg producers. The only problem was, that every egg that we ate for the next week or so, had tiny skulls and crossbones on them and made us hack up dust balls—but none of us ever had lice!

Mom took egg production very seriously, so if the numbers were down, she set out to find the slackard hen who wasn't pulling her weight in eggs. Mom waited until evening when all the hens had their pajamas on and were tucked in for the night to make an unannounced inspection. Flashlight in hand, she pranced back and forth in front of each chick suspiciously. Hen eyes bulged while chicken sweat ran down their beaks. They had been through these inspections before and knew that this could mean only one thing—the egg count was down and heads would roll. Literally!

Mom guided the light up and down the row, looking for nice healthy red combs. They were the ones doing their jobs, but the least bit of a faded comb was the tell-tale sign that someone was goofing off. More than one old biddy had been found huddled in the corner with rouge in one wing and a blush brush in the other, trying to fool Mom, but to no avail. Quicker than anyone can say "Jack Frost," Mom grabbed the offender by the leg and shut her in a crate for the night. At sunrise the next morning, Mom marched the poor critter up the hill, gave her a blindfold and a cigarette and asked if she had any last clucks.

A block of wood with two nails driven into it and a hatchet were the weapons of Mom's choice to end the life of the miserable, free-loading chicken. No sympathy or welfare from my mom. Each carried her own load. Again, no exceptions. She did, however, have mercy on the culprit. I assure you that "Fowl Heaven" was entered quickly and painlessly.

As if the act of separating head and body was not disgusting enough, what came next completes the picture of barbarism at its most grotesque form. As soon as the red-combed topknot hit the ground, kittens from every side of the house came running to claim the prized head. Darling little kittens turned into green-eyed monsters, spitting and hissing at each other. The head was passed from one kitten to the next until one cunning little fuzz-ball got smart and snagged the snack by the ruffle of feathers around the neck and ran like the wind to a hiding place, leaving the rest of them sniffing the ground for chicken brain tartare...if, indeed, chickens have brains!

While that was going on, Mom held the still-flapping body by the feet until the decapitated hen had flapped her last few flaps. Then she handed it to one of us while she went into the house to retrieve the bucket of scalding hot water that had been heating on the stove, previous to the execution.

Although wet chicken feathers stink, *scalded* wet chicken feathers smell worse, if that is possible. It's a smell that one can never forget. As soon as the bird was lowered into the bucket, steam rose and the smell permeated every part of our being, from head to toe, and it didn't leave after we finished the job. It had the staying power of a skunk, so plucking had to be done quickly and methodically. Wanda picked the legs, I, the back and breast, and Phyllis, the intricate parts. It is amazing how many feathers can be pulled by little people when oxygen is denied! Handful after handful of feathers were plucked and thrown on the ground, well... preferably on the ground, but ninety-nine percent of the time, my handful landed on my bare feet along with Wanda's ninety-nine percent! When the chicken was naked, Phyllis took her to Mom, Wanda split, and I was left to pick cold wet stinky chicken feathers off my feet.

While I was cleaning myself, the undeniable smell of chicken hair being singed (and we ladies think that waxing is painful) off the corpse over the open flame of our gas range by Mom, wafted out of the kitchen window right toward me. By this time, I had stopped thinking of the hen as a murder victim and started to think of her as dinner. Let me tell you this, Colonel Sanders KFC has nothing over Mom's MFC.

Mom—always busy!

Foxy Loxy

Our chicken coop was downhill and quite a way from the house. The nightly trip there to gather the eggs and secure the building to prevent foxes from getting in and snacking on our fat hens never got any easier through repetition. I dreaded to see dusk come, which meant that it was time to go face those tiny-headed, overstuffed bags of feathers, with beady little eyes and a bright yellow-orange knife where their mouth should be.

The coop was quite a nice building, by chicken standards. Daddy always had it nicely painted on the outside. Mom kept the manure shoveled and fresh straw strewn over the floor as needed...too nice for those ingrate hens. All that was required of them was a few fresh eggs a day. For upper-class fowl housing, it was a steal.

With one eye on the setting sun and one on the last chicken to enter her abode for the night, I started to quiver with fear. What if a PMS chick was in the mood to peck at my eyes or draw blood? What if a fox were waiting behind the coop door ready to pounce as soon as I touched the knob? Or what if the sun went down completely before the eggs were gathered and I made it back to the house with all of them in tow? Who knows what could happen if any of these scenarios came to pass?

I summoned my inner strength, slipped the handle of the egg basket over my arm, and reluctantly made the trek down to the dreaded "coop."

Although Mom did what she could to keep the smell down, chickens are chickens, and the aroma—even at its best—could knock the socks off of a giraffe. And then there were the evenings when it had rained all day long and the chickens were soaked to their underwear. The stench was intolerable. Nothing like wet fowl!

I'd take as deep of a breath as humanly possible before entering the ammonia factory. My throat burned, my eyes watered. Nonetheless, in I waded, bare feet and no chemical warfare gear. My gag reflex was tested each time I stepped into a pile of fresh doo-doo. I must say that I developed quite the constitution over the years. It enabled me to change diapers when our babies came along!

I sized up the workload. A dozen or so wooden boxes laid on their side in a row against the wall. Each box opening was covered with a burlap cloth, which concealed fresh clean straw, making a cozy little nest in which each hen was to deposit her rent for the day, no exceptions.

I approached the first box with caution and carefully slid my arm in, hoping not to encounter anything but eggs, but always fearing the worst, say a black snake or two curled around the fruit of the bird. Nest after nest had just eggs in them, much to my great relief.

The chickens were lined up on the roost, oblivious to anything going on around them, but there was always one plucky old biddy who decided that she was going to hatch the eggs that she had just laid. But, by Mom's command, I was to gather each and every egg and bring it back to the house, no ifs, ands, or buts. There she sat, feathers ruffled, purring a warning signal, piercing eyes fixed on the would-be egg-napper, and that sharp little knife-like appendage, aimed and ready for attack. It would be a battle of wits.

I tried slipping my hand gently under her, quietly reassuring her that everything was going to be fine. She wasn't buying what I was selling and lit into me like a match in a firecracker factory. I tried to distract her, it didn't work. She was determined to keep the fruit of her labor. I stepped back to think. She just ruffled her feathers and started to sharpen her beak on the roost, never once taking her glaring eyes off me.

Lest you think that I had forgotten about the pitch-dark that was quickly coming, I assure you that I hadn't. I took my eyes off my adversary just long enough to see that I had very little time to complete my mission. Do or die. Protecting my eyes from certain blindness, I grabbed the beast by her scrawny neck and flung her across the building. Amidst chickens squawking, wings flapping, and feathers flying, I grabbed the last egg.

Meanwhile, some of the flock who'd been awakened to a cataclysmic state had started to form a posse, while the rest of them were busy stirring up a lynch mob. I had to move and move quickly. The dust hung thickly in the air as I made my getaway and slammed the door behind me.

My heart was pumping like an oil derrick, but the worst was yet to come. The trip up the hill still lay before me. As the leaves fly before a hurricane, so, too, did I, puffing and panting all the way. I could feel the fox's hot breath on my heels. I never looked back and my legs didn't stop moving until I heard the lock on the back door click behind me. My nerves were shot and the eggs in the basket were already scrambled for breakfast the next morning. I couldn't bear the thought of ever doing that again, but all too soon, it was tomorrow night.

Birds of a Feather

My grandparents kept a flock of gray geese for as long as I can remember. Once in a while, a mother goose to-be would refuse to sit on her nest long enough to hatch the next generation. On one of these occasions, Mom brought home a big fat egg and announced that she was going to hatch it, which conjured up a funny picture in my head of Mom sitting on a goose nest, crocheting little webbed feet booties. She set the egg in a bowl and went into her bathroom, soon emerging with a box and a heating pad, cord dangling behind her. So, this was how all this birds and bees stuff worked!

Pad in the box, egg on the pad, Mom turned on the heat and rotated the egg every so often. I think that that pad must have been on high because it surely didn't take too long for the gosling to break out of its shell jail, and he came out sweating! And as the theory goes, the first one that is seen by the hatchling is its mother, so we girls and Mom were indeed mother to him. He was dubbed Gooty and followed us around like a little bitty puppy.

Gooty spent his days outdoors, playing in the sunshine with us. At night, he slept under a metal-slatted milk crate. One morning, before Gooty was set free, a terrible storm came up. In the midst of the thunder and lightning, Phyllis remembered the goose and ran out in the pouring rain to save the little fellow. She came back soaked to the skin, goose in tow. She quickly handed him to me, but with all the excitement of lightning bolting around the room, he landed tummy side up in my hands. Just as I noticed his position and started to turn him right side up, a loud crack of thunder crashed across the farm like the sound of a B-57. I jumped and squeezed the poor little guy like a tube of toothpaste. Gooty goo shot straight up into the air. I made haste putting him down and ran into the bathroom—upchucking my breakfast. I don't know who cleaned up the mess, didn't care. It's one thing stepping in goose poop outside, but entirely another wiping it out of one's eye. I learned a valuable lesson that day, don't ever hold a baby goose upside down in the midst of a bad storm. This information may come in handy someday.

Sorry to say that poor old Gooty didn't live a full life, but the life he lived was right up there with the Roosterfellers. Since the day he'd hatched, he was cuddled and kissed by each one of us girls. One of his favorite things was a neck rub administered by anyone who happened by. As soon as a hand wrapped around his long, gorgeous gray-feather column of a neck, a soft "gunk-gunk" chanting noise escaped from his trumpeted beak and continued on until he sank into a deep hypnotic state. His eyes barely open and his head hanging ever so slightly was the position for the duration of the massage. The moment the manipulation stopped, he emerged from his trance and was once again his own saucy self.

Hatched on a heating pad and mothered by a gaggle of giggling girls created a slight identity problem for our handsome "now going into puberty" goose. Since chickens were the closest to his species, he decided that he was one. This was not problematic on its own, but instead of fashioning himself after the roosters, he chose the feminine sex and went with it. Jealous of the hens that had a nest of eggs of their own, he decided to kidnap a brood of fuzzy, yellow Bantam chicks from a mother, who in turn flew at him with such gusto that she knocked him backwards into a spiny castor bean plant. Ownership established, a mother-chicky-sitter relationship was formed and all seemed well until a semi-truck came down the road and honked at the unusual goose- Bantam family, which Gooty perceived as a threat. The goose became enraged at the sound of an intruder thundering through his territory. He ruffled his feathers and ran so fast at the truck that he launched himself into flight. Unfortunately for him, the young driver slowed to see such a sight and Gooty ran smack into side of the cab. To make a long story short, the goose was dead, the driver was devastated. Unbeknown to us, each time the truck driver made the trip down our country road, he teased our mascot with his truck horn, causing Gooty to take flight to protect his interests. The man pulled his truck to the side, apologized, and with tears in his eyes, buried our heating pad hatchling. Our handsome prince in shiny gray feathers was no more. He will be missed, always.

Amen

Ouch!

Mom and Dad worked tirelessly at their small truck patch that they planted in the spring, and each fall a bountiful supply of vitamin-chucked veggies were harvested. Big tubs of fat red tomatoes floated in ice water, waiting to be washed, scalded, peeled, and quartered for canning for the upcoming winter.

Mom and Dad surely weren't lazy, but we girls surely had to carry our loads, too.

Picking sweet corn scared me to death. There's nothing quite like walking through neatly-planted tall, lush corn stalks, when an arm happens to brush against a corn worm. And when you didn't even know things like that existed. The first time that I was stung by one of *them there critters*, I thought that I had been shot! A searing pain raced down my arm to my fingers, then up my arm to my armpit, then down my body to my toes, then back up again, followed by cold chills and a strong urge to spew. And this was all in the first second of the sting.

Bug, wasp, bee, mosquito...insect bites in general were always a dreaded part of summer for me. No matter how careful I was not to step on a bee, one would always be lurking beneath a blade of grass just waiting for the opportunity to make my next two weeks a miserable existence. Wearing shoes would have been the solution to most of my pain, but did I ever consider the possibility that putting something between my foot and the bee would have made the difference? Summer after summer went by with at least one two week bout of swelling, itching, throwing up, and pure agony. Who ever heard of allergies? And medication that would have alleviated some of the torture that I endured? Certainly not me. And so, I suffered.

Mom always knew when to do an extra-good job of cleaning the house. This was the sequence of matters concerning bites. I would get stung, throw up, swell, fling myself on the couch, elevate my foot, while trying to hold an ice pack on the sting.

Within the next three hours my mom's cousin and family from Pennsylvania arrived unannounced. I swear those people never once saw me upright. All the kids took off and played, leaving me inside to wallow in my grief. I'm telling you, it happened every summer, but at least Mom had a clean house from the forewarned bee-announcement of their visit!

Picking berries was a chore that I dreaded as much as picking corn. Usually things ended up the same way! Phyllis, Wanda, and I were sent up the hill to pick blackberries so that Mom could bake one of her delicious pies. Believe you me, that pie was the only motivation that would have gotten me out of the house and into the heat, humidity, and work of climbing that hill. And then there was always the risk of spotting a snake or a bee. That was about the limit of scary things on the farm, but just the thought of being accosted by one of these monsters was enough to set my heart into overdrive.

Phyllis and Wanda enthusiastically hustled to their destination while I was only in this for the eats. I was always a good thirty steps behind those two when it came to what I considered *work*. Up the hill, I plodded until Phyllis yelled back for me to get a move on before a black snake decided to swallow me whole. That got me moving. I ran the rest of the way to the berry patch, passing them on the way.

Berry pail hooked over my arm, I waded into the midst of the brambles. Huge clusters of shiny blackberries hung thick on the bushes, but just like picking cherries from a tree, the biggest and best ones are the ones that are the hardest to reach, so deeper and deeper into the center of the brambles I pushed, unhooking the stickers from my clothing and skin as I went. In the meantime, my sisters were merrily picking and singing as they encircled the patch instead of climbing into it. Their buckets were starting to spill over, while I only had a smidgen of berries on the bottom. Then again, they didn't eat as they picked, so, of course, they had much more. Phyllis made up a little song about me that soon Wanda was chirping, too. "Three berries I picked, *do doot, do doot,* in only one hour, *do doot, do doot!*"

Rage welled up in me, as did the heat. I would show them. Sweat started to roll down my brow, which was a signal to all the nearby mosquito and their relatives, that dinner was now being served. Trying not to be distracted from the task at hand, I pushed ever forward until I reached my goal. Never had my fingers been so nimble and quick. The largest and sweetest berries in the patch were mine. I deserved a larger portion of the pie, no doubt about it. Maybe this wasn't so bad after all. Perhaps Mom would even give me two pieces. I picked faster, ignoring the chanting in the background. The temperature must have been in the mid-one-hundred and twenties, but the thought of those pies was a driving force. I fell into a picking trance. Doing so caused me to let down my guard. I made one giant push for the final ten berries in the middle, when, WHAM. I was hit on the right, then on the left. Then the right again, three more to the left. My worst fear was being realized. I had stuck my hand into a yellow jackets' nest. I never knew that a sound like I omitted could come from human lungs and vocal cords. I threw the bucket straight up in the air, berries fell like ebony raindrops, as the whole center of the patch started to move like a washing machine set on heavy load. I was only concerned with getting out of there with my life, no matter if I had to leave my hair and skin behind. I crawled my way out as my sisters watched in amazement at how fast I could move. I'd gone into the patch looking like a normal kid and came out looking like Quasimodo's ugly twin. I would have won the Blue Ribbon for the most grotesque costume at the annual Halloween party. I was covered in blood, sweat, and tears. Holes were ripped in my clothes and my head was swollen three times the size of a kid my age. I had been to war and survived to tell it, although, it was a few weeks before my lips were deflated enough to utter a word. The pie? Well, let's just say, I didn't care who got the larger piece!

Wanda, Phyllis, me, and Mom

Phyllis, Wanda, and I in front of the world famous "Longaberger Basket."

Deck the Hall

The smells of Christmas hang vividly in my sinus passage memories. Two weeks prior to the Jolly Fellow's arrival, the house was cleaned to surgical status. The menu had been planned, cookies baked, and, of course, the most important thing...a letter to Santa was written, pleading amnesty for all the devious deeds that were committed during the year.

Being too young to write for myself, Phyllis volunteered, and so with pen and paper in hand, she lovingly guided me to the kitchen table, lifted me onto the chair, and grilled me about my Christmas wishes. With every item that I mentioned, she informed me why I shouldn't, couldn't, or wasn't going to get it. We finally agreed on a gray crayon and a used piece of string. Sounded good to me and so the letter was written, signed, and sealed. Now for the delivery.

I was instructed to follow her to the mailbox, which happened to be in the basement. Dutifully, I shuffled close behind her. As we neared the landing on the staircase, I tried hard to remember if I had ever seen a mailbox down there, but I knew there had to be one. She told me there was.

We walked a few steps more, when Phyllis came to an abrupt stop. We stood in silence. Surely, we had not reached it yet. I looked to my left and then to my right. Nothing. Then I looked in front of me. We were standing in front of the furnace. Or, what I thought was the furnace. Silly me! All this time I thought that this was a furnace, but, it was a mailbox! I didn't question. I just watched as she opened the letter chute. I was a little alarmed when I saw flames dancing around the post office! She grabbed the letter out of my tight little fist and tossed it into the fire. I became hysterical as I watched my carefully-crafted letter disintegrate, right in front of my eyes. I started to wail until Phyllis patted me on the head and explained to me that the smoke from the letter went up the chimney and straight to the North Pole. How foolish I felt. Of course, she was right. My sister would never do anything to sabotage my Christmas! I remember thinking what a wise woman she was. However, I was a little concerned that the smoke would be intercepted by some crusty, little old man in Canada who couldn't have cared less whether Santa came to my house or not. I just had to wait and see. In the meantime, I had to be good...very, very good.

The two weeks before Christmas were brutal. Every kid I knew was on his or her best behavior. For me, it was very difficult. Threats from Mom came at regular intervals, "You'd better be good or Santa won't bring you anything!" Then Phyllis reiterated the same thing, only worded as a hint to Mom and Dad that maybe I really was bad and I didn't deserve anything. I tried to avoid Wanda. She was an easy target to steal things from or to make squeal about anything and everything.

Two weeks seem like an eternity, but finally Christmas Eve arrived. It was time to get a tree. Every Evergreen that was shaped like a triangle was prime target for country folk, no matter whose property it was on. I don't know where Dad got the tree, but on the Eve, a fresh-cut tree was brought into the living room with a wooden "X" nailed to the bottom of the trunk.

It was set in front of the double windows and readied for bedazzlement. Daddy meticulously arrange the lights on the tree and hoped all would light after being connected to an electrical source. If one bulb was out, all of them were. The job of finding the burned-out bulb was time-consuming and frustrating. We girls stood behind Dad as he checked each light, periodically asking him how long it was going to be before we could see the beckoning lights that signaled the arrival of the most glorious time of the year. Finally, success! Each and every tree, year after year, was more beautiful than her predecessor.

The bubble lights were my favorite. I could stand for hours watching the bubbles rising and falling in their glass vials, but, alas, one could not stand for long in front of the tree for fear of getting radiation burns from the heat of the bulbs. Now, I understand why the tree was never up longer than a week. By the time we took the tree down on New Year's Day, great scorch marks lay under each bulb and needles fell like a monsoon rain in Asia. Let's just say, it was a lot skinnier going out the door, than it had been coming in.

Mom slaved in the kitchen while Puddles, our Manchester Terrier, sat at her feet for handouts. Scents of all kinds of baked goods permeated the house. We three sisters hung every priceless (to me) ornaments on the tree. No more than a few dozen slipped through our fingers and crashed to the floor. Fire crackled in the fireplace as buckeyes exploded from the heat. Dad sat contently in his big, brown armchair, smoking his pipe. This was Christmas Eve at our home. Warm, safe, clean, busy, and full of love. No one came over. It was just the five of us. I loved every minute of it.

Daddy helped us put cookies on the plate and milk in a glass, then sugar cubes for the reindeer on a stand beside the tree. We scurried in to get our baths and jump into bed before miniature hoofs were heard clicking on the roof.

It was hard to fall asleep, but Mr. Sandman finally arrived and sprinkled his magic sand in my eyes, and I was out like a burned-out bulb.

Morning came, my eyes opened, and I didn't hesitate. I was always the first one to the tree. I was always the first one to take a quick check of the cookie plate. Yep! Santa had been there and what a sloppy eater! There were crumbs all over the plate and table, but no cookies. Well, of course, he didn't have time to be neat. There were millions of homes to deliver presents to, and millions of cookies to be eaten. And no wonder only part of the milk was drunk. Surely, he had to be bursting at the seams. Rounding the table on my heels, I caught a glimpse of the tree. Presents were everywhere! I plopped my butt down on the floor and started sifting through the packages, tossing this one and that one to the side, scratching and tearing at each one labeled with my name.

Wanda and I almost always got the same thing, only a different color. Mine, a boy's blue, hers, the most delicate shade of pink. Such a feminine and petite color. I never opened a gift, of which I was not insanely jealous, because she always got the prettier one.

I never was fond of dolls, but on this Christmas morn, I opened a package that had the most breath-takingly beautiful dolly that I have ever seen, even wearing blue. Wanda's was still prettier, but I was satisfied. Daddy prompted me to fill her bottle with warm water and feed her. I ran to the kitchen, got the water, and anxiously returned to nourish my new responsibility.

Gently, I picked her up and cradled her in my arms and, to my amazement, she drank the entire bottle. No sooner was the last drop gone, when my lap started to feel warm and wet. I picked her up to see just what the matter was. Pee! She had peed on me! What a dirty rotten thing for her to do to her new mother! I jumped up, flung the doll across the room, and started to gag as I ran to the bathroom. Daddy sat in his chair slapping his knees, howling with laughter. Some sense of humor! Well, that did it for dolls and me. I'm sure glad that piddlin' babies didn't repulse me when I got older. I would have been in real trouble as a mother!

Soon all the gifts were opened and I was dry again. No worse for the wear. As if opening our gifts were not stimulating enough for me, the best was yet to come. Christmas dinner! Ham, turkey, mashed potatoes, gravy, dressing, cranberry sauce, candied sweet potatoes, corn, beans, peas, bread, fruit Jell-O, and cakes and pies of every kind. A feast made for a king. Mom always made enough to feed an army.

This was one day that we could eat as much as we could, and as often as we wanted. And I, for one, was not going to pass up that opportunity. Mom's sour cream pie was to die for and I could clean up an entire pie by myself. Each of us overindulged.

Once the wishbone was broken, the turkey tail was eaten (Mom's favorite), and the carcass laid bare, it was time to clean the afterglow. Phyllis and I were assigned that task. She washed and I dried. This was our nightly duty, so the kitchen game that pursued was routine.

Phyllis was positioned at the sink and I stood on a chair. The rules of the game were simple, I had to shut my eyes, open my mouth, and swallow whatever she put into it. The object was for me to guess what it was that I had just gulped down. Assuming that all was edible, which really was presumptuous on my part, I readily agreed to her bidding.

Delicacies ranged from mustard on pineapple chunks to peaches in tomato juice. She had a blast thinking up weird combinations, and one with a much more delicate stomach than I, might be apt to pitch up her gourmet concoctions.

After a few duds of taste tests, I started to balk at her game. To draw me back in, she promised to give me some cotton candy. Cotton candy! Was she kidding? I would have crawled on my hands and knees across the Sahara Desert for cotton candy, and she knew it. Being the trusting little soul that I was, I foolishly opened my mouth into which she popped her version of this fine confection.

At first, it was quite sweet, not bad tasting—a little pithy. I rolled it around on my tongue for a while, tried and tried to swallow it. "T'was a bit dry," I thought to myself, but I just chalked it up to a lack of culinary experience on her part. Finally, down it went. It felt like a hairball was caught in my throat. Coughing and wheezing, mucous membranes activated, and tears running down my cheeks until it eventually slid down my esophagus. The commotion caused Mom to materialize in the kitchen. The game was called, when Phyllis's recipe was revealed. A cotton ball dipped into the can of sugar! And this was the sister I trusted to send my letter to Santa via furnace!

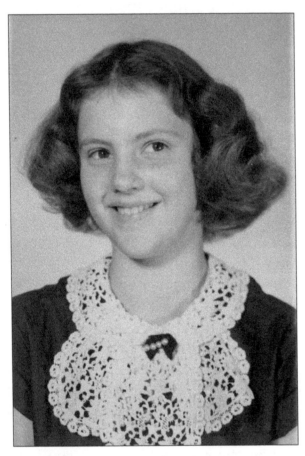

Phyllis, Santa's personal secretary!

O' . . . It'll Be All Right!

In our household, there was absolutely no reason to go to the doctor's, unless one of the following occurred:

1. Life's blood was spurting from every pore.

2. Fever was over 110 degrees.

3. An eye, ear, or limb was not attached to your body.

If any of the above was moved to another location, or it was still hanging on by a strand of skin, then the doctor's office may or may not be considered. Depending on how thick the strand was.

An abscessed tooth was not even looked at twice. Even if it was chronically abscessed, and pus squeezed out every time pressure was put on it. A *front tooth*, nonetheless.

Every morning, when I brushed my teeth, I'd pop the pus bag on my gum and then went on with my day. But, on the days when the pus was oozing from my tooth and swollen like a blood-filled tick, and the pus bag was pushed halfway out of my gum, just lying on my lower lip like a ripe banana hanging off a tree...well, then it was almost too much to bear. A real trooper, I went to school anyway and suffered in silence, constantly holding one hand over my mouth so as not to freak everyone out. Mom's response was, "Oh, it'll get better." It didn't seem to faze anyone but me, that I could have gotten brain damage or even died from such a small part of my body. Going to band practice to play my trumpet was excruciating, let alone nasty-tasting. That was my first brush with death.

The second was caused by me. As I'd stated before, if there was a furry animal in the house, I could not leave it alone. A hibernating one was no exception. My sister's boyfriend had gotten her a de-stunk skunk as a present, if that tells you anything about my (now) brother-in-law!

The skunk was in his cage out back and had been in a deep sleep for about a month. I figured picking him up and cuddling him during this time would not cause any harm. After all, it was a warm January. What would be the harm of waking him for just a little while?

Supposing the little stinker was in an anesthetized state, I wasn't particularly careful about how I stuck my hands into the cage to grab him. He must have been a really-light sleeper, because the moment my hand touched his fur, he uncurled and sunk his front teeth into my left thumb.

I seriously doubt that a rattlesnake bite could have been any more painful! I unhooked his teeth from my thumb, locked the cage, and sniffled my way into the bathroom where I administered first aid. Alcohol. It burned like the devil, but I assured myself that all would be fine.

I tried to forget about it, which was a total waste of energy. No forgetting about this. I went to the school dance as planned that evening. Midway through the gala, I glanced down to my now-throbbing arm. Instead of just my thumb, I was alarmed to see that there were red, feverish-looking streaks running up my limb. I cut the festivities short and went home. I fessed up to Mom about what had happened. I was in such pain. Her response, "Oh, it'll get better."

I was one sick puppy, but after a week, it did get better. I had dodged another bullet!

My third such encounter was not exactly a near-death experience, but a loss of a body part *experience*. High school was okay for the most part, but since I went to a very small country school, supplies and teachers were not of the finest quality. (I can say this now. Most of them have passed on to the great chalkboard in the sky.)

We were given new scalpels in Biology class to dissect frogs. Little did I know that I would be on the receiving end of the blade during a small flirty altercation with one of my male classmates. He called me a wussy little girl, so I slapped him. He defended himself by raising his scalpel. The slap was executed and my little finger landed smack on top of the blade. I pulled my hand back and my finger was severed to the bone. I took one look at it and down I went. The next thing I knew, my teacher, who was the football coach, young and cute, was carrying me up the stairs to the office.

We didn't have school nurses in residence, so the secretary patched me up the best that she could and assigned another student to walk to the doctor's office with me. Those few blocks seem like a few miles, but I made it. Doc stitched me up and sent me back to school. No one bothered calling my parents. We were tough back then!

Mom didn't have the opportunity to say that *it would be fine*, nor did she have the say of whether I would go to the doctor or not. After all, it was hanging on by more than a strand. If the rules for doctor visits was followed this time, my pinky would have been hanging half on, half off, until it dried up and fell off like a lamb's rubber-banded tail. Thank goodness, the decision was made by the school secretary-nurse.

I have absolutely not one athletic bone in my body. Lunch time was a nightmare for me. Intramurals. During the winter months we played dodgeball. It was mandatory. Not all the jocks in school were guys, but there were several gals who had arms the size of Schwarzenegger's and could throw balls as fast as bullets. And they all came gunning for me, especially one of my best friends, who thought it was funny to see me run. I had an awkward gait and tripped over my own feet most of the time, so I was an easy target for her. Try as

I might, I could never catch her balls and always ended up on the bench.

One day I got the audacity to really stand up to her. She had humiliated me for the last time. I braced myself for every ball that was thrown my way. She took notice of my different approach and stood back and gave everyone else a chance to kill me. I was catching the balls left and right, dodging here and there. Then she saw that it was up to her to take me out. She hauled back her throwing arm, got me in her sights, and let go. I had my eye on the ball. It was coming straight at me, full force. She held nothing back.

I started to dodge, and then decided to run backwards. I don't know who or what gave me the idea that I could run backwards, when I couldn't even run forward, but I did. Before the ball hit the target, I tripped, falling hard to the floor. My head hit the hardwood like a ripe melon.

As I lay there, analyzing the damage that was done, I wondered…was my brain still intact? I wasn't sure. Again, coach scooped me up and carried me to the office. This was getting to be a habit. I just wish that I could have enjoyed it!

I suffered a concussion and was told to rest for forty-eight hours, but there was a school dance that night. Mom let me go. She was sure it was *going to be all right*. After all, there was no blood and the bump was only the size of my fist. "O', It'll get better!"

Fire! Fire!

Art Linkletter once said that kids say the *darndest* things.

Well, I don't know about that, but I do know that they *"do"* the *"dumbest"* things! After going through two days of intensive fire prevention and safety training at our school when I was in the 4th grade, I had the distinct opportunity to teach my kid sister, first-hand, all that I had learned in that time.

For whatever reason, I will never know, nor will I know how we escaped Mom and Dad's attention, when we decided to make clown faces out of candle wax. But, there I was, with red, blue, and green candles in one hand and a book of matches in the other. It was a beautiful warm, windy autumn evening. The last few lightning bugs of the season flitted past our noses. Moths were dancing happily in the glow of the back porch light. I handed a candle to Wanda, struck a match and—with a whiff of sulfur, we had fire. I felt a little guilty, lighting a match without permission, but after all, didn't I know all that there was to know about fire safety? How dangerous could a little ol' candle or two be?

I struck another match, lit a candle of a different color and handed it to the kid. Her hand shook as she reached for it. It was obvious that she was inexperienced in this area. I was about to teach her the ins-and-outs of true face painting. The medium? Hot wax! I watched as the wax puddled around the burning wick. Just as the wax was ready to drip over the edge of the candle, I carefully lifted it over my head, tilted my face towards the moon, and tipped the candle just enough to let small drops of boiling hot color fall onto my face. Painful? Yes! But, wasn't a great looking clown face worth it? The red dots were placed methodically and skillfully. Now for the blue ones!

Wanda cringed as she watched me endure pain while perfecting my masterpiece. Never had I seen her so enthralled with a project of mine. I had captivated my audience, and rightfully so. Was I not suffering for my art?

One wick steadied against the other, I lit the blue candle from the red and set to the embellishment of my work. Starting from one ear and tilting my head to the side so that the color could follow the contours of my face, I smiled inside at the thought of how intricate this masterpiece was going to be, when my thoughts were interrupted by Wanda's hysterical scream. "Wow! This must be better than I had imagined! I can't wait to see this in the mirror!" Again, my thoughts were interrupted when out of the corner of my eye, I caught a glimpse of orange and gold traveling up one side of my hair, which had been newly home-permed by my mom, who had not one ounce of beautician blood in her veins. If the directions for the perm read to leave the curling solution on for twenty minutes, then, surely, forty would be about right.

I watched out of the corner of my eye as fire quickly climbed the hair fodder that is so lovingly referred to in the Bible as "a woman's crowning glory." Dad taught us that there was always a way to resolve every situation...once it was correctly diagnosed. I was fairly certain that I had called this one right—my head was on fire! The solution, oh yeah, put it out! What an opportunity to teach my kid sister all that I had learned from my fire safety training. And I could use this as an excuse to explain to Mom and Dad why one side of my hair was gone. What I wouldn't do for my little sister. Teach her how to stay safe, no matter what the sacrifice to me! They would surely believe it. Now back to the solution. Now let me see...is it stop, drop, and roll? Pat it with my hands to smother it? Dip my head in a bucket of water? Oh, yes! I remember! Shake my head fiercely and run like the wind to get plenty of oxygen to it. That did it! Now instead of a small ball of fire, it had turned into a raging inferno! I shook my head until my brains rattled. By the grace of God, a big gust of wind came just in time, putting the fire to rest and saving one half of my lovely perm.

It was over as quickly as it had started. I stood, reeling from the shock, eyes wide from the horror, with smoke rolling from my ears. I ran my fingers over my still-smoldering head. Where dry and brittle, over-processed curls once were, crispy stubbles now stood in their stead. Wanda and I stood in silence, looking at each other in disbelief. What had happened? Was it a dream? Wanda slumped to the concrete in a heap and quietly began sobbing.

Reality set in when Mom called us indoors. There was no lying about this one. We were playing with matches and there were tell-tale signs of our misbehavior. Fried hair and the distinct smell of singed fur. We hung our heads, swallowed our tongues, and slowly slinked into the living room where Dad had taken his favorite chair for the evening. Upon getting the first whiff of our deed, Dad looked up from the evening newspaper, caught a peek at me, and started to laugh hysterically. Mom, on the other hand, did not see the humor, and lit into us with the standard, "You kids don't have a lick of common sense," speech that was delivered without fail each and every time that we were caught not using a lick of sense!

I was sent to bed, as is, even though I begged to wash what was left of my coiffed mane. And so, it was that I went to school the next day smelling of smoke and brimstone. Lesson learned! It was a whole year before my hair was long enough for another "Lilt"!

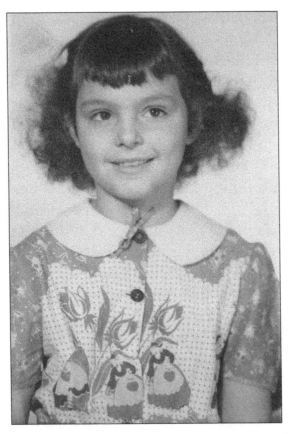

One of Mom's infamous "Lilt" home perms. Notice the bangs!

My Grand Music Debut

With all the professionalism and finesse of Leonard Bernstein, I approached the lyre, trumpet in hand, I confidently raised it to my lips. This was the night that I would shine. This was the night that I would make Mom and Dad proud, the night a new star would be born. I nodded to the accompanist. Not a difficult piece, but quite lovely. I had it memorized, had gone over and over it again in my mind. I'd drummed the timing out with my fingers for weeks on end, had practice until the notes rang forth as smoothly as liquid gold.

As far back as I can remember, I have loved music. Deep in the core of me, music has quickened my soul. Perhaps the trumpet might not have been the best choice of instrument to pronounce my heartfelt love for the note, but it surely could herald forth the exuberance I had in my spirit.

I remember the day that our music teacher announced that a professional musician was at school to help those of us who were interested in joining the band, to pick instruments that we were best suited to play. After trying several without success, including biting a clarinet reed in two, I settled on a trumpet.

I could hardly contain myself on the way home. How I approached Mom and Dad would be crucial. I knew that they would consider a program, such as this, frivolous. I was prepared to beg. Excitement oozed from my every word as I talk to them that very evening. My presentation must have gone fairly well because I was told that they would think about it. They would have a decision by morning.

As I lay my head on the pillow that night, visions of a marquis with my name flashed across my mind's eye. I would be famous, I was sure of it. Visions turned into dreams and soon morning arrived. I bounded out of bed to receive the decision. To my utter amazement, not only did Mom and Dad decide to let me have a trumpet, but we would buy one rather than rent. But it had to be a used one. Fine by me. My own trumpet. My music teacher happen to know of a trumpet for sale, like new. And it was, too! It was beautiful! Long, slender, shiny, a tone as crystal as a bell. Fifty dollars. What a bargain! The money was taken out of my bank account, saved from my fifty cents a week allowance. I was now broke, but it was worth every penny. She was all mine. We would go places together.

So here I was, standing in front of the school auditorium, ready for my grand debut. I wet my lips, position my fingers across the keys and waited for the last note of the intro. A couple more notes from the piano. I pursed my lips— golden notes would ring fourth. The accompanist glanced at me

with a reassuring look and I looked back with con-
fidence. Here it comes, the first perfect note of my
perfect career. My fingers clutched the trumpet
ever so tightly as the audience patiently awaited
my performance.

The time had come. I pressed the mouthpiece
tightly against my lips and gave a blast of air—
BLAH!!!!! I couldn't believe the hideous noise that
resounded through the auditorium. I started to
shake, I got dizzy, the room was spinning. My fingers had a mind of their own. They kept hitting the
wrong keys which were now sticking in the halfway
position. I couldn't breathe. There was no air in my
lungs to force into the mouth piece. It couldn't have
gone worse if I had tried!

I glanced over the lyre and saw people snick-
ering all across the room. Mom and Dad had slidden
as far down in their chairs as possible, which for my
6-foot 4-inch dad was not an easy task.

An eternity later, my debut was over. I couldn't
take it back. Red-faced, I wobbled back to my seat.
How was I ever going to face anyone ever again,
let alone Mom and Dad. I finally gathered enough
nerve to look around at them, hoping for a " we love
you, anyway "smile. They had slipped out the back
door. They turned tail and ran. They never came
to another performance that I was a part of. But in
all fairness to them, there weren't that many other
times. Fear had taken over and my days of getting
up in front of a crowd by myself were very few
and far between. My love affair with my trumpet

ended that night, but it still stands in my corner, laughing at me each time it catches my eye. BLAH, BLAH, BLAH!!!

Dead Cat Walking

One great fear in my life is *dead animals*. It doesn't make much sense, I realize, but nonetheless, if I see a dead animal, be it large or small, squashed on the road or dead of natural causes, a panic wells up inside of me that I can't explain—or maybe I can.

Every spring, Mammy Cat presented us with a new litter of kittens, much to my delight. She must have had some reputation, for Tommys from every farm in the approximate area would appear out of nowhere bearing gifts to woo her. She wasn't too picky. In fact, she wasn't picky at all. She ended up with kittens of every color, shape, and form. There weren't any DNA tests back then, so it was a guessing game trying to pin paternal rights on any one of these slick gigolos with certainty.

Her choice of hospitals was one of the many buildings on the farm. She usually chose the barn. That's where most of the animals went to birth their babies and, besides, there were a lot of rooms from which to choose, plus bales and bales of hay. I loved going into the hay mow to check for newbies who might have fallen out of their beds or wandered away from Mammy on their wobbly little legs. The smell of hay wafting in and out of my nostrils caused me to sneeze uncontrollably as I crawled from bale to bale, pausing briefly on each to listen for tiny distress calls.

Halfway up the mound, I stopped short. I positioned my body across the bales and peered deep inside the pile. Yep, it's a fur baby, all right. The expectation and excitement of finding a new, soft baby kitten grew as I slid my small arm into the crevasse that a kitty would call home. I couldn't quite reach it, so I slid forward a little and thrust my arm in deeper. Oh, there it was, a small warm, wait, did I say warm? Much to my horror, it was not warm, nor was it small. I gave it a poke. One or two more healthy pokes confirmed my suspicions, a dead cat! I yanked my arm out of the abyss quicker than a flap of a hummingbird's wing. I ran up the hill, screaming my lungs out for Mom. She armed me with a paper bag, a rag, and orders to dispose of the body, which I knew was to swing it over the neighbor's fence into the woods. I had seen it often, especially the year that distemper broke out on the farm. I knew it wouldn't be hard to locate the burial grounds since I was sure that there were many cat skeletons that marked the " X ."

I reluctantly shuffled down the path to the barn, humming my own little dirge. I entered the doorway, looked at the stack of bales, and hesitantly started my ascent to the scene of the crime. Well, how did I know that it *wasn't* a crime? After all, there was a body! Cold sweat ran down the back of my neck as I approached my destination. I stared into the dark—where the body was entombed.

Darn! It was still there! My whole being went into a full systemic shiver. The very thought of touching something dead was as repulsive as it got for me. Let alone there might be a snake in there. This was dangerous stuff!

I finally summoned the nerve to slide my hand down and across the body to make an assessment of the situation. Yep, it was dead all right. Cold as a cucumber that has been in the fridge overnight. As I mentally checked off the names of the felines that I had not seen for a day or two, the big black barn cat, Blacky, came to mind. I struggled to move the hay to expose the corpse, keeping an eye on it to make sure that it did not move. Cold sweat had now turned to hot sweat as I pushed with all my might. The obstacle was moved just enough to expose Mr. Cat.

On occasion, surgical extraction of a stiff was required where the bales had to be cut and separated, just to get a handle on the situation, but, if the tail was in the upright position, removal was relatively easy as long as the extractee didn't weigh more than the extractor. I reached for the rag that Mom had given me as a deterrent against dead cat germs. I pulled it from the elastic around my waist and wrapped it around poor old Blacky's tail. I got a firm grip and gave it a yank. Nothing. I tightened my grip, gritted my teeth, and pulled with all my might. *Nothing.* I released my hold, sat down on one bale, and positioned my feet on another and gave one last pull. At this point, I was not thoroughly convinced that he was dead, but, with all the stirring to get him out, the stench of death left no doubt of his demise. The smell was overpowering. It was now or never. Wretch, pullll! Wretch, pulllll! Wwrretchhhhh, the body went flying across the hay right onto my lap. And from the smell of him, it had been a little longer than a day or two since I had seen him. I jumped up and the cold, stiff, smelly cat hit the floor like a ton of bricks.

I composed myself. Again, I wrapped the rag around his tail, dragged him across the floor to the mow opening, and with my bare foot, gave him a hefty push. I couldn't bear to look, but the thud was unmistakable—he was down.

Now the real tasks lay before me, that of transporting the body, then the burial. I climbed down, once more grabbed his tail, and started the procession. He seemed to be much longer in death than he had been in life, might have been because his front and back legs were locked in *extend mode.* I struggled to lift him, but his head dragged the ground. I took a few steps. He dropped to the ground. I tried not to look at him. I just knew he was alive, in spite of the smell. I gathered him up yet again, but, this time I started to sing, loudly, so as not to hear his cries for help. I was shaking all over. Finally, with one jerk, I took off across the field, running as fast as I could, his head thumping and bumping all the way. I don't know how long it took me to reach the makeshift cemetery. Maybe the heat of the hot, August day made it seem longer, but, surely three days had elapsed before I made it all the way across the field. But, finally, I made it.

Now what was the difference between *our side* of the fence and the *neighbor's side* of the fence? It was just a place for a dead cat's body to decompose. I don't know, but there must have been some reason, or Mom wouldn't have told me to throw him over, which was no small feat for a small child. I propped the body against the fence post, climbed up the fence, reach down to grab the deceased 's tail, still not allowing my eyes to fall on his, just in case he was looking back. It took me several minutes of tugging and grunting to get him hoisted to the level of release. I felt like a Mafia clean-up man. He hit the ground with a hollow thud, and with that the burial ceremony was over. No pomp, no circumstance...certainly not clean and tidy. Nonetheless, finished. I threw the rag over after him. I gave another big shiver and high-tailed it across the field. Nightmares depicting Tommy cats chasing me ensued for weeks afterward.

I've thought back on this incident several times in my life and wondered what it might be like at the end of my life. Most people refer to it as "passing on," when I know full well and good that we do not *pass on*. We are just "thrown over!" I just hope that more dignity is shown for me than was shown for that poor cat!

Where's Andy?

I don't know when Andy came. I don't know from whence he came. In fact, I don't know who he was, where he lived, or what he looked like—yet—I had contact with him every day of my young life. He was as good of a friend as any could ever have. We had countless hours of playtime and he was always welcomed. Every tea party we ever had, there was a place of honor set for him, and not once did he ever disappoint us by not showing up. He was punctual, courteous, and quite entertaining. A delightful guest.

He was Aunt Jeanie's best bud in the world. Although, most times she laughed at his antics, there were times that he made her cry, which was always upsetting to me. Those were the times that I wished he would leave, but, given a little space, soon she would be laughing again and right back to the party at hand.

You see, he was a figment of Aunt Jeanie's imagination, but, the day in, day out, play time with Andy made him as real to me as any person clothed in flesh and blood. I never once doubted his being.

The party house was an old, empty corn crib with wooden slats on the sides and a tin roof, that when rain hit, made the most hypnotic sound. Still one of my most beloved sounds in the world. Through the slats, we could take in the sights, sounds, and smells of the farm. Geese and ducks waddling up and down the lane, and kittens catching crickets and crunching them down like kettle-cooked popcorn. On a hot day, sweat ran down our noses and into our teacups. The wasps and flies buzzed so loudly, that at times it was maddening. But on cold days, the wind blew through the slats with gusto, and we pulled our coats tightly around our necks as we sipped our tea. The pretend scones were always perfectly baked and each day we had a different flavor.

Aunt Jean was the youngest child in my mother's family. Born with Down Syndrome in a time that families shoved them behind closed doors and pretended that they didn't exist. Not so with Aunt Jean. In her younger years, she went to square dances and all the social gatherings in the farm community. She was quite the caller of square dances, in her own way, "a turkey wing and a turkey wing!"

She spoke in a whisper, usually spoken *past others*, as if she were speaking to someone or something of another world or dimension. Not understandable to mortal adults, but to little kids, it made no difference. We knew exactly what she meant.

She was short and round and had long, black stick-straight hair, that hung down her back in neat braids. Mom took great care of her sister. Each morning, Mom made runny, soft eggs smothered in ketchup, and buttered toast to dip into them. It was disgusting to watch her dunk the bread and dribble egg yolk across her plate, over a dish towel that was tied around her neck, and finally over her chin on the way to her mouth. I believe this is how egg facials came into being. A cup of coffee washed it all down and she was good until noon.

The only time I remember hearing a sound out of her other than soft whispers, was when Mom deemed it necessary to give her an enema. Then all heck broke loose. She screamed, like a banshee, at the top of her lungs. Usually a docile person, she'd turned into a raging bull, with the strength of two. All the while Mom is doing her best to insert the apparatus without drowning both of them. It was quite the sight to behold. I'll spare you the details, but let me say, the ketchup soaked eggs were no match for this!

Aunt Jean had a dolly in her arms at all times. She wrapped and unwrapped her doll, in a soft blanket, hundreds of times a day. Neatly and tightly, like a burrito or a fine Cuban cigar. When she colored or drew, the baby was laid on her lap or placed snuggly beside her. She spent hours writing letters (to Andy, I suppose), of neat little squiggles, page after page. She never ran out of anything to write.

I was never embarrassed of Aunt Jean. She was unique and different, the way God intended for her to be. I am so glad and proud that she was part of our family. I learned many things from that dear little soul. Tolerance, patience, love, and most of all, imagination! Thank you, Aunt Jeanie, and Andy, wherever you are!

That's A lot of Horse...Manure!

There were horses on the farm. Not sleek, fast, beautiful ones, but big ol' fat-butted draft horses with clip-cloppy hooves that could cripple a kid with one misplaced step. They were awesome to look at from a distance, but to get close to them was absolutely terrifying. Not only were they tall and wide, with heads the size of small cars, but, their feet...well, their feet were fascinating. Huge and fluffy—and *huge*. I only approached them when they were in their stalls and all I could do was look at their feet. The few times I pulled my eyes away from their peds and allowed myself to gaze at their muscular haunches, I was in awe.

Day after day, I watched these monstrous beasts march up and down the rows of earth...plowing, pulling, planting, and harvesting field after field of corn, wheat, barley, and hay. I admired how their heavily-muscled bodies shown in the summer sun as the sweat moistened their dark smooth hair. What magnificent animals. Well trained and obedient, responding to every command. Their Commander, my red-headed German-Jew Uncle Kenny, was one of Mom's brothers. He was a few years older than she.

I loved my uncle Kenny. *Why?* I often questioned myself. I didn't know. He was a self-absorbed stingy man concerned only with his own well-being and wealth. He shared nothing and took (legally) everything he could, for himself. In the same way Aunt Jeanie looked past us when we spoke, so did he. Only for different reasons. He didn't care about anyone's problems, news, or conversations. It was all about him and his possessions. A gigantic wad of chewing tobacco could always be found, stuffed in his cheek like a greedy chipmunk. Slimy, brown tobacco juice ran from the corners of his mouth and down over his scraggly, unshaven chin.

His attire was always the same: denim work pants, boots, and blue chambray shirts; appropriate dress for a farmer, but on each and every one of his shirts, and on each and every day, he wore his favorite piece of jewelry. A large heavy diaper-like safety pin. Pinned securely to his left breast pocket sat this huge pin that reflected the sunlight with his every move. What was its purpose? My best guess was that, in his thinking, it was the lock to his excessively-swollen private vault that made his pocket virtually impenetrable to mankind. An exaggeratingly-full vault, stuffed with as much cash as a pocket could hold. Not content with tens or twenties, he'd cram the pocket with large denomination bills—a wad the size of Kansas. That pocket bulged to the point of splits city. If even one small piece of lint were added, it would have popped like an overly-ripened zit!

He opened the vault several times a day, either to rummage through it or to brag about its contents to someone. Inside were bills...many, many bills. He carried fifties and one hundred-dollar bills, all neatly folded and pressed to the max. To his dying day, that's how uncle Kenny carried his money. I have no idea why he was never bumped off or mugged. I can tell you that in today's society, he would not have died a natural death! It amazes me to think back on his crude security system, but it worked!

And just as secure as his money was his stash of candy, which he kept hidden in his bedroom. On one of his rare generous moments, Uncle Penny—my son's name for him—offered Wanda and me a piece of candy.

We climbed the curved staircase and entered a small, dark room with one bed and one dresser. As our eyes adjusted to the dimly lit space, Uncle Kenny crossed the room, and stood in front of his dresser. He cautiously glanced left and right and then behind...checking for any unwelcomed intruders who might try to discover his candy fortress. Satisfied that all was secure, he slid the drawer halfway open. He stuck his arm in up to his elbow and rummaged through his underwear and pulled out a long work sock. Reaching deeply into the toe of it, he extracted a small bag of burnt candied peanuts. Wanda and I gasped with delight. Not only were we getting a piece (and I do mean a piece!) of drawer candy, it was also "sock" candy!

What a treat! He hesitantly, as if he'd had second thoughts about his uncharacteristic, unbridled generosity, handed us each our peanut, which we gleefully stuffed into our mouths and happily skipped down the stairs, never ever to be offered another precious piece of DSC (drawer sock candy). What a great guy!

He was not selfish with everything that he owned. Occasionally, he'd offer me a gift from his *Mail Pouch* chewing tobacco pouch. Not a good, juicy leaf, but a hard nasty stem that was not supposed to be in the package in the first place. But since it came from Uncle Kenny, I thought it was delicious. I chewed on the stem until it was non-existent. Not much juice was extracted from one stem for me to spit, but I tried my best!

What few curse words that I ever heard came from him. Not the raw, indecent words that we hear today, but "damns and hells" sprinkled with a few "sons of b's." It sounded like pretty rough language to me.

Uncle Kenny never had a driver's license, never drove a tractor, or ran anything mechanical. Everything was done by horse. If he needed to go into town, he hitched a ride with one of his farming neighbors. He never took a vacation, hardly ever went off the farm. Every now and then, he went to Pennsylvania to visit a close cousin. He had one hobby—coon hunting. He would take off on foot, late at night, with a flashlight in one hand, his gun in the other, and his coon dogs at his side. The next morning, I would see him out in the field or down at the milking barn, like clockwork. His life was simple.

A more negative man I have never met. Never a compliment or nice word about another human was ever heard coming out of his mouth.

There have been times in my life that I would catch myself thinking that I was better than another, when the thought of Uncle Kenny would pop into my mind. After all, the same blood that courses through my veins, ran through his. It is quite humbling. But I loved him!

My Mom

My mom was the pluckiest little woman I have ever known. She stood not quite 5' 4", a whole foot shorter than Dad. She was never afraid of work, or getting dirty. She could confront when confrontation was called for, or face fears of any kind. I counted on Mom to get things done, to find lost items, or come up with solutions to problems. I never knew Mom to be afraid of anything, either. Mom would handle the situation.

I've seen her get out of the car, step into traffic on the 5th Street two-lane bridge, take a hammer—her tool of choice—from the back floor of the car, open the hood, and beat the devil out of our old Nash to get the transmission into gear. She never paid "no mind" to the rush hour traffic that was tied up both ways on that narrow bridge. I was always afraid that she wouldn't be above taking that hammer to anyone who challenged her to "move that car!"

No air conditioning in those days just added to the misery. We couldn't shut the windows to block out the honks and shouted profanities. We kids just sat in the car, red-faced from the heat and embarrassment, stuck in the middle of the bridge, watching Mom throttle the heck out of whatever part she thought wasn't working.

Mom's mechanical knowledge came from living on the family farm with several brothers. That would have been okay, but, being familiar with horses does not a mechanic make. She could throw bales of hay along with the best of them, but needless to say, horses don't have transmissions and motors, so pretty much she didn't know anything about newfangled *'chines*. What she did know, she used wisely. What she didn't know, she guessed. Sometimes it worked and sometimes it didn't—but if it didn't fix the problem, it wasn't because she hadn't given it at her best effort.

I've seen her wrestle cows, chickens, pigs, horses, dogs, and cats to give them medicine. I've seen her pick objects up that were heavier than she was. She's moved stuff that was not humanly possible for a man, let alone a five-foot, four-inch woman. I've seen her repair things with rubber bands, tape, string, and pins—and they stayed together. They knew better than not to!

I've seen people twice her size back down when Mom got her dander up. What a woman!

But, there was this one time.

One beautiful spring night, right before I graduated from high school, Mom and I decided to take a walk. Our route took us past the country cemetery that was adjacent to our home. I walked that path frequently in the daytime, but it terrified me to walk past it in the dark. But, Mom was going with me, so nothing to fear. There were no street lights and very little traffic.

"No Fear Fanny" and I started out at a pretty good clip. We had to get the heart rate up, of course. I cringed as we walked past the first few drives of the cemetery but relaxed as soon as we had passed it. With the graveyard behind us, we turned our attention to the sky and to the beautiful blanket of stars above us. Out of nowhere, four iridescent green lights appeared right before our eyes. Two rows of two. One light above the other. Like a box. They were moving simultaneously and slowly across the sky. We both stopped in our tracks and stared into the star-saturated black of night. I had, and have never since seen a color of green like that. Brilliant, shimmery, almost like round balls of gas. I'm sure both of our mouths were hanging open.

We didn't say a word. Just as fast as they appeared, they were gone, moving at a speed that was incomprehensible. A "swish" and they were gone. Mom and I stood there for a split second, doubting what we had seen. We look at each other when Mom said, "Let's get out of here!"

Those words that I had never heard uttered from my mother's lips tore right through my soul. She was afraid! I was terrified! We ran all the way home. Heart rate? Well, it was up, alright!

Although the fear has diminished a bit after all these years, the memory of that color has not dimmed at all. We took no more night walks after that. For months I couldn't bear to do more than just glance at the heavens after dark. As far as I know, I have never been abducted by aliens, but, periodically, I check my belly button for any suspicious marks. One can never be too sure!

Mom and I standing in front of Dad's barber shop.

Mom and I eating dessert after a big meal.

My Daddy

My dad was a character, without being one. The eldest of seven, he quit high school after his Junior year, so that he could financially help his family. Times were tough in the country, so many young sons never graduated from school for the same reason.

He joined the army and served three years Stateside and was due for discharge, when World War Two broke out and he was called overseas for three more years, never saw his homeland in such. He left an infant with his wife and went off not knowing if he would ever see them again.

He served in the European Theater and spent much of his time in Iceland. Even though I was not born at the time, I sorrow over the circumstances, not just for Mom and Dad, but for all of our servicemen.

Upon his safe return, rather than coming home to a wife and infant, he returned to a long legged, skinny, four year old. He declared that he would never leave home again and he stayed true to his word. We never had a vacation. Occasionally we took day trips to the zoo, fairs, lakes, and lots of picnics.

After Dad's love for God and family, his country came next. He was a member of the VFW and served as Chaplin. He volunteered to safe keep the flag, to be responsible for its flight and folding at day break and dusk, and protect it from getting wet. Our home was adjacent to the Veterans Park, and many were the times that one of my sisters or I would be summoned to "Get the flag" before the rain came, if he was busy cutting a patrons hair. I came home more than once, soaked to the skin, but the flag was nice and dry! We learned respect for our flag and our country from that dear man. God has blessed this land and I pray that He will continue to do so. Thank you, Lord, for my wonderful, beautiful home! United States of America!

Dad was quiet, I think deep in thought, most of the time. He had no sons, only three noisey girls. No one to really talk to, so he somewhat isolated himself from us. Of course, there were times that I helped him in his woodshop, where I learned a wealth of knowledge about tools, measurements, etc. Dad was a teacher, always. Mom taught us about nature, wildlife, and such, but Dad taught us common sense. I have a whole head full of his warnings and sayings that I have tried to pass on to my children and grandkids.

He was OCD, without a doubt. He was meticulous about everything. "There's a place for everything, and everything has its place". Mr. Clean, all right.

Dad had a weird sense of humor. Like the time he drew, in ink, a stupid-looking picture of my principal on the envelope of my report card that had to be turned back into the office every 6 weeks. I nearly had a stroke. Our head honcho at school had no sense of humor, and I knew that I would get a week of detention for that. No way would he believe that my dad had drawn it. "Nothing but blatant disrespect", but Mom came to my aid and covered it with a flowered sticker. Disaster averted. Dad just laughed and laughed.

Dad budded and grew into a flower after his salvation at forty-five years of age. He talked and interacted with us more. I think perhaps, the Lord healed some horrors of war for him and he started to let go. He turned from being a soldier of the USA Armed Forces to becoming a soldier of the Cross. Every Thursday, without fail, when Mom and Dad went grocery shopping, Dad put on a crisp white button-down shirt, a bow tie, with a little KJV New Testament tucked into his shirt pocket.

As soon as he entered the store he took a seat on the window ledge by the cash registers, pulled out his Bible, and read the entire time that Mom shopped. I assure you that he was noticed by each customer as he or she came in or went out. It was the way he testified that he was a born-again believer, and was ready to give an answer to any and all who had a question about the Word.

My Dad loathed bragging and lies. He was an intelligent man and a man of integrity. I knew if he told me something, it was the truth. I never doubted him. I gave Daddy a kiss every night on the forehead, and a kiss was returned on my cheek. I miss him, but I will see him along Mom's side, someday soon.

Dad— always with his Bible.

Dad's idea of a joke!

Still Looking Through the Binoculars

I adjusted the lenses on the field glasses and focused in on my childhood church. A small country church with stained glass windows and a huge bell in the belfry, where it hung. I remember the men taking turns pulling the rope to herald the beginning of the service and the echo that resounded through the tiny community. It was the only church around, so if you were a church goer, that's where you went.

I especially enjoyed all the Bible stories. We learned the songs that went along with each story. I had no doubt that every word of the Bible was true and still to this day, I believe everything that is written in that dear book.

I must have been five or six years old when Mom and Dad decided that we three sisters were old enough to be baptized. Contrary to what I believe now, we marched forward where the "Reverend" dipped his hands into a bowl of water and doused each of our heads with it. He then pronounced us "saved." I didn't understand a thing about it, except some guy had just ruined my hairdo!

The three of us marched back to our seats, Mom and Dad beaming with pride. I remembered thinking, "What was that all about?" I spent the rest of the service wiping the water drips out of my eyes and patting my head dry trying to salvage whatever was left of my "do."

Fast forward ten or eleven years to when I was sixteen years old. I'd started to get pretty mouthy and disrespectful to my parents. Most teenagers do. I knew it was wrong...but *knowing* and *doing* the right thing does not always add up to the same conclusion. I felt guilty about my disrespect towards my parents and realized that I was sinning against God. What, you mean I am a sinner?

The thought scared me to death because I remembered the verse, Romans 6:23 "For the wages of sin is death, but the gift of God is eternal life through Jesus Christ our Lord."

The wages of sin *is* death? Well, I knew that I was a sinner, and I hated it. I hated the guilt. What should I do about it? I pondered for a while and then the verse, Ephesians 2:8-9, "For by grace are you saved through faith, not of yourself, it is the gift of God, lest any man should boast." I knew exactly what to do. So, in the fall of my sixteenth year, a senior in high school, I asked God to forgive me of my sins and asked the Lord Jesus into my heart and He became my Lord and Savior that very moment. I never looked back. I knew my sins were forgiven and gone forever. Not just my past sins, but my present and future ones as well. I was now a child of God, forever. Heaven is my home.

The Big Apple

Each year, right before graduation, it was customary for the high school seniors to take a class trip. Projects to earn funds were conducted throughout the last three years of high school in which each student worked to contribute money to the "kitty".

Candy drives were the easiest to pull off because everyone wanted to buy big fat chocolate bars for a buck each. What a bargain! We divided into groups, walked our small town streets, knocked at each door, and sold our goods. We never went by ourselves. It was a very small town, but one can never be too cautious.

Four of us decided that we were going to take a Thursday night to canvas the area, so, I went to the first friend's house to pick him up, and then we were to both walk to the other two classmates houses to join them. My friend was not ready by the time I arrived, so his dad asked me to take a seat on the sofa to wait for him. I obediently did so, but was quite uneasy since he and I were the only two in the room. He started to make small talk as he intentionally plopped himself down close beside me.

He was a huge man, perhaps six four or five and approximately 260 pounds. He was a businessman, certainly not a redneck, so, before this day, I had never feared him. He was a friend of my dad's, well, more of an acquaintance than a friend, but nonetheless, a man who didn't seem to be a threat.

He moved even more closely, if that were possible, and the first thing I knew, he threw his massive left arm over my shoulder, pulled me close to his chest, reached around me and with his hugh hand started to fondle my breast.

I was frozen with fear.

I didn't know what to do. Time stood still. I can still see the couch, the room, the amount of light around me. I can feel his huge body and the heat from it and the weight of his arm on my shoulder. And the way he looked at me. It makes me tremble even now as I write this. It made me physically sick to my stomach.

I immediately jumped up just as my friend entered the room. I'm sure he wondered why I was red-faced and shaking from stem to stern. I never told him. I didn't tell anyone. I was ashamed and embarrassed. Why is it that the victim is the one who carries the guilt? I'm sure this event was the driving factor of my working for the Child Abuse Protection Program; to teach children how to handle a situation like that or worse.

I never told my dad. I told Mom not long before she died and I told my husband around the same time. The secret had been hidden inside of me for years. I can't imagine what it is like for a child to suffer far greater abuse.

It was a few years after I was married that the man died. I was glad—really glad, but God gave me the grace to forgive him, which I did. If he is in Hell, I am sorry. I wish that fate on no one. However, unless he repented of his sins and asked the Lord to be his Savior, Hell is his home. Forever. Earthly pleasures are short lived.

The details of the class trip were sown up and the "kitty" was divided equally amongst thirty-six classmates. Each of our bags was packed and we boarded a train headed for the "Big Apple". It was 1964 and we were going to the World's Fair. Most of us had never been out of the state before, so this was a momentous time in our lives.

For weeks before the trip, I ran around the house singing, "If you can make it there, you can make it anywhere. It's up to you, New York, New York!"

I wasn't on the train for more than 5 minutes until I was busted for squirting lemon juice in one of the guys' eyes. The problem was, that while aiming at my target, I shot the teacher in the eye, also. I didn't get off to a very good start!

I don't know how I missed this, but I guess there was a car full of young soldiers behind us. Some of my classmates were fraternizing with them, but, of course, I missed out on the whole thing! I certainly didn't spread my wings too far on that trip. After all, that would have meant that I would have had to leave the car that I was assigned to. Always have been a little pedantic.

We stayed at the " New Yorker Hotel" and were divided into three to a room. Of course, we had picked our roommates beforehand, so there was no fussing at the last moment.

I have never had a smoke or a drink in my entire life, and this trip was no exception. While nearly everyone was out late doing whatever they were doing, my best friend, Susan, and our other room-mate were all tucked into bed getting our beauty sleep for the next day.

Honestly, for only being there one week, we got to see many of the sites of the city. The Statue of Liberty, Empire State Building, the Rockettes at Radio City Music Hall, St John's Cathedral, Central Park, Skid Row. We even saw the playground where West Side Story was filmed. We were on our own in New York City in the night. We all found our way back to the hotel safely. Amazing!

Towards the end of the week, we went to the World's Fair. A massive piece of land with all kinds of pavilions and buildings with newfangled gadgets of all sorts. Everything was automated. Even some of the walkways.

We stood in awe as we admired Michelangelo's pieta. There were those who were bowing, crossing themselves, crying, and praying. "People, it's just a piece of marble"—but, it was beautiful!

We had Belgium Waffles with strawberries and whipped cream. A new cola was introduced and handed out as samples. "Tab". I thought it was deli-cious. There were people from every part of the world at the fair. Somewhat like Walmart is today!

I was standing in a line of one of the exhibits with my friends, when I noticed a really good looking, Continental guy glancing my way. He and his friends shuffled a little closer, as did I. I think we realized at the same time that we did not speak the same language. So we did the next best thing. When it was time to go into the pavilion, we positioned ourselves so that we would be sitting next to each other.

Taking our seats, we lean toward each other, and put our arms on the same chair rest, so that they were slightly touching. It was the best we could do. But some languages are universal, and I believe that we were speaking the same. We were both taking in each other's aura. We walked out of the theater together, gave a final look, and walked away. Never spoke the first word to one another, but, believe you me, the message was loud and clear!

The week was an unforgettable one, etched in my mind forever. On the way home, I went to the back of the train, and stood on the platform of the caboose where I was joined by a buddy of mine. In the dark, we listened to the steady rhythm of the wheels as they passed over the rails. We talked about the future. It was so strange to talk about a future that would not include the people with whom I had spent the past twelve years. My classmates, my brothers and sisters. The very ones that I had seen nearly every day for that amount of years, would not be included in my daily life here after. An honest sadness came over me.

Don went back to our car . There I stood in the blackness of the night listening to the click-clacking of the train, feeling more alone than I had ever felt in my life. I was an adult. I would be facing the world in that light from now on. It was an overwhelming emotion that encased my very soul that night. I would go on without my childhood friends.

On the train, traveling to the "Big Apple"

My friends at the 1964 NYC World's Fair

Frazeysburg High 1964 graduating class

Twelve "perfect attendance" certificates. Congratulations, to me!

My New Life Begins

One of my friends, Wanda, and I were cruising around town, just for fun. We pulled into the "Beverly," for a quick burger and fries and waited for the carhop to bring them out. The car was pulled forward where we looked directly into the dining area of the restaurant. Sitting in a booth were two guys finishing their burgers and shakes. Eye contact was made between the five of us and giggles started to escape our lips as we glanced their way, every once in a while, and vice-versa.

They finished and laid down the tip, came out the door, and got into the convertible right next to us. Of course, there was more giggling and quick glances from each party.

Both of the guys were tall and good-looking, not bad for a Saturday night's trip into town. They opened their car doors and slipped into their seats. The one that I was interested in was the owner of the car, or at least he was driving. He put the key into the ignition and gave it a turn. Nothing. He tried again, same thing. Red-faced, he climbed out of the car and approached ours. I was delighted! He stumbled over a few words and asked if we could take them to his house a mile or so down the road. You could never do that today, but we allowed them to load into the back seat and off we went. We exchanged as much information as we could during the short ride, but all I know was that I really honed in on the driver's beautiful green eyes and long eyelashes.

We made the trip to the house, picked up jumper cables and delivered the cables and guys safely to the disabled car, where they jumped it, and then, *poof*, they were out of our lives. We talked about them for several weeks. I couldn't forget those eyes!

I was dating someone at the time. A weight lifter, whose eating habits put mine to shame. Such clean eating, not quite the fare that I wanted at that time of my life. But, I still couldn't get that night out of my head. A tall, good-looking guy, with a beautiful convertible, (all right, so it needed a jump every now and then! Nonetheless, it had potential). And so did he.

My final year in school droned on and soon he was shoved to the back of my thoughts as I participated in senior activities. Graduation came with one big accomplishment. I had completed eight years of grade school and four years of high school with perfect attendance . Something that I had prayed for as a child to accomplish. God was listening to me even then.

Summer arrived. Mom and Dad always went into town to do grocery shopping every Thursday like clockwork. I had nothing to do on one of the shopping days, so I decided to tag along. Big Bear was their choice of stores, and as luck would have it, there was always a bunch of college guys who worked there doing the summer to help finance their next year of school. Wasn't any harm in checking out the line of stock and carry-out guys. Yeah, yeah, I know, I was still dating Mr. Muscles, but, again, no harm in looking.

I went to the bread aisle to pick up a loaf for Mom. The guy who was stocking the shelves turned and bent down to pick up a flat of buns and looked up at me. I couldn't believe my eyes, nor could I ignore his...Mr. Green eyes himself!

I think that he was as delighted as I was to have met again. We exchanged niceties and parted, but you can believe that those Thursday morning shopping trips became a habit for me that summer. I couldn't wait until we were out of groceries. I think I ate twice as much, just to get back to that store.

That fall, Dad decided to try another church. We went in the morning to the new one and on Sunday evening, we went to our old one. I decided to ask Mr. Muscles to go to the new church with me on a Sunday night, which he did. We walked into the chapel, and low and behold, who was the first person I saw? Mr. Green eyes! I was shocked. I had been going to the morning service and he had been going to the evening. This was looking better all the time, and so was he!

Now, don't get me wrong. Mr. Muscles was no slouch. Tall, muscular, tan, good looking, and smart. He had it all, but the heart is a funny thing and mine was beating after the hunk of gorgeousness with the beautiful green eyes, who later became my husband. What a darling!

Now that we knew that we attended the same church, we started to go at the same time. Larry gave his heart to the Lord Jesus that very same night. He was nineteen, I was seventeen. We were both now children of God and so baptism was our next step in our relationship with Jesus. Baptism is our outward sign of identification with Christ. His death, burial, and resurrection. A few weeks later, we were immersed in Baptism in the same service. He waited for me after the service and asked me out for our first date, but, I already had one with Mr. Muscles. My Dad was beside himself with the prospect of my dating this new Christian man and could tell that I had feelings for him. He advised me to let Mr. Muscles go and not waste his time, which I did.

Mr. Muscles was a great guy and it was an amicable break up, but I knew where my heart was headed. And this time I understood baptism. No more water on my head, just the precious blood of my Savior that cleansed my soul. My life was starting to come together. It's awesome how the Lord works.

My first roses from "Mr. Green Eyes".

My gorgeous soldier!

Lar at Fort Gordon, Georgia

Lar, home on leave.

Lar and I at one of my art shows.

Larry and I at a washed out hot-dog roast. That's soda, not beer!

Pulling grapevines with a little friend. I love nature!

Closer in Time

I dare not look at my life as a whole...but focus on wee chunks here and there that have surfaced. For the sake of not straining my brain, I am fast forwarding through my marriage, my children, and all the errands and demands that go along with that era.

As an empty nester, I found myself bored and unproductive in all areas of my life, so I decided to accept a position as an art instructor at our local YMCA for the summer. Teaching lifted my spirits and I, once again, was happy and had joined society. My schedule of Tuesday, Wednesday, and Thursday mornings each week was just the right amount of stimulus I needed to help me out of the abyss that I had fallen into. It was challenging planning different projects for kids four-years-old to sixteen, but interacting with the different age groups was fun and entertaining. Classes filled with thirty or more children kept me on my toes. Most sessions ended with more paint on me then on the canvas. One thing for sure, only old clothing was worn so as not to sacrifice anything good to the Painter Gods. I never wore my jewelry to class. Too messy. I'd spent much too much time cleaning my diamonds to have them dunked into pots of color.

I left them at home. One morning, after I had finished cleaning my art room and had nothing else to do, I decided to take the day to shop. The full day! My house was spic and span and I was caught up on all my chores, so instead of turning right for home, I turned left and off I went for a relaxing day of browsing through whatever shops that I chose. Footloose and fancy-free! I'm not one for shopping for personal things like clothing and the such, but oh, oh, how I love to shop for items to decorate my home. Each piece that was purchased was placed in a specific place that I had in mind and never moved. Somewhat like in a museum. OCD? You bet! Never could I have imagined right at that precise moment that my life would be changed forever. I wouldn't know until I walked into my immaculate home after my shopping spree.

I paid for all my packages and started home, hoping that I had left enough time to get there before my husband, who had been golfing all day with a buddy. As a wife and mother, it was instilled in me that I should always be home before anyone else so that I could have dinner waiting for them. It is a habit that is hard to break. I pulled the car into the garage, gathered all my new goodies and stumbled in through the kitchen door, trying not to drop anything. I laid the packages on the floor and pushed the door shut with my foot, with sort of a backward kick.

As I always do when I entered the house, I admired its cleanliness and beauty. We had it custom built and it truly was a beautiful home that sat on six acres of heavily-wooded land on the edge of a gorgeous ravine where the wild animals jumped and played on the forest floor. My favorite? The dozens and dozens of wild turkeys that climbed up the hill each and every morning just to peck at their own images on our downstairs doors and windows. Many a time, I sat at the exit of our New Hampshire look-alike driveway and waited for those birds to cross. There were several clutches hatched each spring and had to learn the rules of the driveway. I counted sixty-seven of them one day and was late for an appointment just waiting for the long-legged goofy looking creatures to cross. I tried leaving at different times of the day just to avoid a traffic jam!

One of the slower turkeys got hit by a car and lay dead in the driveway. Although I felt badly, I really wanted his tail feathers to put in a fall wreath, but, no way was I going to pull the feathers out of that bird. He laid there through the night until I could figure out how I was going to ask Larry to "harvest the crop." The next morning, I drove down the driveway to figure out a solution. Problem solved! Some predator had eaten the entire carcass and only the tail feathers remained. There were no bones, joints, or toes. Just tail feathers! Enough to make my wreath. Voila! Waste not, want not!

I hung the finished wreath on our front door. I loved it! The next morning, as usual, his fellow turks marched up the hill. As they rounded the corner of the house I noticed that they stopped and stared

Poor Turkey!

at the wreath, as if they'd spotted something very familiar to them. They immediately took a head count, called a group meeting, and set post at the door. It was weeks before I got enough nerve to exit through that portal. There were some mean-looking Toms who stood guard, but turkeys are easily distracted so it wasn't long before their attention was averted by a June bug, and they went AWOL.

Coming in second were the big, fat red squirrels that bombarded our propane tank with freshly-picked acorns. Quite the entertainment for them! Sausage was the prince of the forest with his sumo-wrestler's physique and gigantic fluffy tail that was the envy of the entire Squirrel Kingdom. The ground shook each time he jumped from branch to branch. He would have made some mighty fine vittles for some redneck and family.

Then there were deer, raccoons, and chipmunks who ate every single tulip bulb that I planted. And the groundhogs and owls...oh, how I loved my owls. Especially in the winter when they called back and forth to each other across the hollow. And, oh yes, my little hummingbirds. Many of my hours were spent out in the screened garden room, watching them fight over the various feeders that were cleaned and sterilized each week to keep the little birdies healthy. Each spring the same hummers came back to find freshly-made food just waiting for their return. Napoleon was my favorite guy. He was really short and fat and sported the most beautiful red vest that I have ever seen on any bird.

Annie was my favorite little girl. Gentle and willing to share her feeder with any who would pass by, unlike all of the other ones who were greedy and aggressive.

I pushed the button to close the garage door and turned my eyes to look across the gigantic kitchen island and was stunned. I mean, really dazed. Standing in the stead of my pristine kitchen, were heaps and piles of desk papers, drawers up-ended, stuff strewn everywhere. My first thought was that something had blown up, but, as my senses came back to me, I realized that we had been broken into. What a mess! I rushed to my desk where I had hidden our vacation money. By the grace of God, they had missed it and took a smaller amount hidden in a different place. Parky Pig was stolen. He only had a couple of hundred dollars in change. I could handle that. And then, my mind went upstairs where all my valuables were. I called the police and then ran up the stairs. Just as I had suspected. Our bedroom was ransacked. A case had been stripped from the pillow and all of my jewelry was gone. Never, ever, have I ever been so sick! Larry and I had been married for forty years at that time and all the beautiful expensive, irreplaceable pieces near and dear to my heart were gone. These were part of our young love. Mom had given me her mother's Art Deco flawless diamond ring. A real treasure and the only thing that connected me to my grandmother. Even a garnet and diamond ring that Mr. Muscles had given to me. Gone, all of it!

By evening, it had sunk in that more than likely, I would never see these pieces again. I can't explain this, but the only thing I could do was pray for the person or persons who had stolen them. $35,000 worth. Not insured. Never entertained the idea that someone would touch my stuff. I prayed and prayed for that person's soul. I immediately forgave him and went on with my life the best that I could.

Several weeks later, he and his pregnant wife were caught while robbing another home. With a small bit of hope of seeing my things again, I sat down and wrote a letter to him. Unbeknown to me at the time, a victim is not to have any contact with the prisoner, but somehow the letter got to him.

"Dear James, please let me introduce myself. My name is Marti Shrigley. I live at 2222—. I believe that you know where that is located since our home was one of the many that you broke into and from which you stole precious things and memories. I am so sorry that this happened. I have trusted others all my life, so this was a real shock to me to have my personal belongings scattered and rummaged through. My clean house was in disarray and doors and walls kicked in. My husband took a chemo treatment that day before he played golf, and I was teaching children's art at the YMCA. I was trying to make a difference in our new community. My husband needed his painkiller that night but it had been taken. The poor man not only was stressed from the robbery but was also in pain, which he had to endure until he could get another prescription filled.

I thought that perhaps you would like to know what you stole along with the pieces of jewelry. My grandmother's antique rings. They were to be passed on to our daughters and then to my granddaughters. It was the only thing that I had that connected me to this dear woman. Granddad had given me six 1800 silver dollars that I had saved for each of our grandchildren. I wanted these passed down the line, also. My carat and a half diamond and wrap that took me twenty years to acquire by trading up every few years. My big black onyx ring with opals and diamonds, my husband bought for me 'just because.' It was a love gift. My engagement ring that was given to me forty-one years ago on Christmas Eve before we were married the following October. A grandmother's bracelet with little crystal figurines that symbolized each of our grandchildren. My pearl ring given to me years ago by my wonderful husband. My amethyst ring that was given to me by a friend from Brazil. My garnet ring that was given to me from my first puppy love. A watch from my mom and dad. Mom is 87 years old, my daddy died when he was 55. It was a graduation gift. My husband's wedding band representing forty years of marriage. And I could go on and on. I won't. I hope you get the picture. Although I am really heartsick over the loss of these items, they are only material things. In Matthew 6:19, 20, the Bible tells us not to lay up *Treasures upon Earth*, where thieves do break through and steal, but lay up *Treasures in Heaven* where thieves do not break through and steal. There is one thing that no one can steal from me on this Earth and that is my eternal life. I trusted Christ as my savior when I was sixteen years old and although you stole from me precious Earthly things, I still have and will have the most valuable thing I possess forever and ever.

And now the real reason that I am writing to you. There is good news for you. You have not done one thing that God can't and won't forgive you for if only you will confess your sins to God and repent of them and accept Christ as your personal savior. We have all sinned and come short of the glory of God, Romans 3:23. Romans 10:13 says for whosoever shall call upon the name of the Lord shall be saved. Just as the thief on the cross beside Jesus was saved to eternal life by accepting Christ as his personal savior, so may you. No matter what you have done. Although I'm not that happy with you now, I have prayed that I would be a part of your salvation by telling you of Christ's love for you. He took the punishment for our sins because sin requires a payment. 'For the wages of sin is death, but the gift of God is eternal life through Jesus Christ Our Lord.' Romans 6:23 It's very simple and FREE! God's grace and mercy are abundant. We all deserve Hell, but we all can escape it by accepting His Son as our Savior. Please, James, for your soul's eternal sake, allow the Lord to work in your life. You are precious to Him and He wants you for his own.

And one more thing—this is for me. I really want my things back. God is able to do this. All of them were on loan to me from him, but I wasn't through with my jewelry yet so I asked him to return it to me. You can help. Out of the goodness of your heart, would you please tell the police what you did with them or who you gave or sold it to. I know this will work in your favorite through the court system. I know I mean nothing to you, but I have been honest with you and no matter what, I will be praying for your salvation and your wife's—and your dear little baby.

Please help me get my things back. Thank you. As His servant, Marti.

P.S., I would like to visit you and explain a little more in detail about God's great love for you and the plan he has for your life. He really does love you. Feel free to write. I would love to hear from you. Marti Shrigley. Address given."

James responded promptly,

"Mrs. Shrigley, first off, I really do commend you for your heart and your courage in writing to me! Secondly, I truly am sorry about the memories that I took from you, as well as the pain and anguish that I've put you and your family through! As of now, my involvement with the detectives is over and any further inquiries or investigations is to go through the prosecutor's office. I have sent word through my attorney that I would be willing to help the prosecutor's office recover some of the stolen property, but only if they are willing to give me a deal that would get my wife probation. I have accepted my fate, but my wife doesn't deserve this! She is as much of a victim as you are! I can't promise you that all of your possessions will be returned, but I am at least willing to help you retrieve some of it. Now, although I appreciate your concern for my salvation and my soul, I'm afraid that those were lost to me long ago! I have accepted this as my fate as well! Once again, I truly am sorry.

James

P.S., if you truly want to pray for someone, pray for my wife and my unborn daughter! Your prayers are wasted on me!"

How sad it was to me to hear of a person's lost condition with no hope...oh, so he thinks. But I know better. So, the letters continued back and forth for a year. But first the court date. It was slated for a few days before Christmas. I sat down and wrote another letter that would be read face to face to him in open court. It was nerve-racking to think about it but I knew it had to be done, publicly.

I tried not to focus on the upcoming day, but rather went about my holiday shopping, cooking, and planning. The day came quickly. I wasn't quite sure what to expect. All of his victims who attended his sentencing were invited into a holding room and briefed as to what we should expect, procedure-wise. As we filed into the courtroom, I quickly glanced around and was amazed at how large the room was. We were seated in the jury box. The gallery was packed. In the balcony, a few shackled prisoners sat waiting to hear their fate, later in the day.

The gavel banged and all attention was on the judge. He spoke for a few minutes, and then turned his attention to the jury box. My heart started to race. The judge asked if anyone would like to speak. I wanted to stay seated but I kept my resolve and stood. I asked the judge if I could face the prisoner. I was given permission, so down I went.

This was the monster that I had nightmares about? A small, frail, very pale, stark-white thirty-three-year old, bald-headed man who looked like a fifteen-year-old kid with oodles of sub-standard tats, ones that looked like they had been done by a fellow inmate. Some, I'm sure, were by his own hand. Lots of them from head to toe! A member of the Aryan Nation since his first year in prison, fifteen years ago, he became quite the student of hate. Half of his life had been spent incarcerated. Even though he was small, he was scary! I steadied my nerves and took a deep breath. The courtroom was dead silent and it startled me when my voice broke the stillness.

"James, as I was decorating the Christmas tree yesterday, I couldn't help but think about you and what kind of a Christmas that you will have. Sadness overwhelms me when I realize that, although you have stolen valuable and irreplaceable possessions from me, you have stolen much more from yourself. You have stolen your first Christmas with your new baby and her first Christmas with her daddy. And not just the first one, but all of her childhood, teenage, and into adulthood Christmases. You have stolen your opportunity to see her take her first step, speak her first words, pull her first loose tooth, to comfort her when she gets her first boo-boo.

You have stolen your opportunity to have a normal family life with your wife and child. How sad. I truly feel sorry for you, but this is the consequence that you will have to pay for your actions. Unfortunately, you are not the only one that is a victim of your crimes. Your wife, your daughter, me, my husband, my children, my grandchildren, and all the others that you have robbed are victims. For me, I have prayed that I would be able to forgive you. I decided to ask you for my things to be returned, and I've decided to turn the whole matter over to God and leave it with him. I have to obey God and do what he wants me to do—and that is to tell you about his mercy and love, his promise of Life Everlasting through his son, Jesus. You have two choices...you can be a jailbird daddy who chooses to make bad decisions. You can choose not to better yourself or make a difference in this world...you can choose to be a dad that your daughter can be proud of. A man of integrity, an honest and decent man, even though you are incarcerated. You can turn your life over to Christ and become that kind of a man. There is not one thing that you have done for which he won't forgive you, if only you will ask. You may think that your life is over, that it is of no use, but God has a plan for you. One of the greatest men in the Bible was the Apostle Paul. He was responsible for many a Christian's death, yet God still forgave him. He became one of the most outspoken witnesses for the Lord Jesus. He was imprisoned many times throughout his life and each time he used the opportunity to tell his guards and fellow inmates about the one true God and his forgiveness.

I have been excited about meeting you so that I could tell you face to face that there is hope for you, there is a full and happy life waiting for you to freely accept. The best Christmas gift that you could ever receive is that of eternal life, just by repenting of your sins and asking the Lord Jesus to become your personal savior. Easy and quick, and forever. Romans 10:13, 'For whosoever shall call upon the name of the Lord shall be saved.' James, I wish you the best and I forgive you. We will talk later."

He never once looked at me.

I stood in silence for a few seconds and then returned to my seat. As I sat down, I looked up to the balcony and noticed a young man, handcuffed, wiping tears from his eyes. Although I was speaking to another, I believe that the message was meant for this young man, too. We may not know whose heart is touched, but God does.

The judge once again invited any who wanted to speak to come forward. The lady next to me stood and walked up front, faced James, and started in on him, but the tale she told was much different than mine and her loss much greater.

Her voice trembled. "You have no heart. You have no compassion. You have no right to exist in a civilized society." And then the tale was told. Her 88-year-old mother had died within a week of the burglary after being told that her irreplaceable family jewelry was taken.

"You made my mother's last week on Earth miserable and sad." She went on to say that she and her husband had one son who was very close to his grandmother and was devastated when he learned of her death. On the day of the funeral, they were waiting for him to appear and when he didn't, they figured that he just couldn't stand the thought of his dear grandmother lying in her casket. Shortly after the service they found out that he had been killed in an automobile accident on the way to the funeral. 'You took the last birthday gift that my son will ever give me on this Earth."

Made my loss seem quite petty. I was ashamed.

She finished and then quietly walked back to her seat. Once again, dead silence.

The judge spoke a few more words and then handed down the sentence. The prosecutor and defense attorneys had agreed on a sentence of twenty years but the judge gave him thirty-three. His wife's sentencing was a few weeks afterwards. She had three years of college completed and both of her parents were school teachers. Not at all the type that you would figure would hang around a skinhead, let alone marry him. Her parents denounced her. The judge gave her eight years. She had her baby in prison. All totaled, both of them had robbed sixty homes. Broad daylight. Armed. So glad I went shopping that day!

Christmas came and went and things started to seem a little more normal. James and I spent the next year writing to each other. I told him how to be saved and as to this point in time, I don't think that he has ever asked Christ to be his savior. His life is not over, though! So, I will keep praying.

This is where my spiritual surgery started. Losing things that I dearly loved. *Earthly things.* I used to sit in church and stare at my jewelry, watching the light jump from one stone to the next. Sounds terrible, I know, but God had to take that love of things from me and I can honestly say now that it was one of the best things that could have happened. It was several years before I got to that place in my thinking, but never once was I mad at God for allowing this to happen. One lesson that I learned from this time of my life is to "Hold loosely to earthly things. We came into the world without anything, and one thing is for sure, we will go out with the same."

More Loss

I finished the summer's art program and accepted a part-time position as a counselor for CAPP (Child Abuse Prevention Program), going from public school to school in our county, teaching children the do's and don'ts of situations that they might encounter. I also worked for an orchard, guiding school children on tours of apple trees and pumpkin fields. What fun! I loved the hayrides and watching the little ones stumble over the vines as they chose just the right pumpkin. Picking a fresh crisp apple from the tree, hearing the crunch, and seeing the juice fly from that first bite is a treat all to unforgettable.

My favorite part-time job was that of decorating a restaurant foyer for a good friend. I could really let my creative juices fly. That made me happier than I had been for a long time.

Mom turned ninety-two in the spring and was doing amazingly well for that age, although we could see that she was tottering around a little more than usual. She still lived in her own home, and cooked and cleaned. Daddy had been gone for years from a stroke that he suffered when he was fifty-five. Mom had one little dog that she loved dearly and a stray cat that came to live with her that she called *Kitty*

Kitty. Mom was constantly busy canning, cooking, making jelly and candy, and it was that way until her last day. She slipped and fell in her bathroom and died that very night of a brain hemorrhage.

Mom was *always* there. What a change in my life there would be. We had a very simple, closed funeral at the cemetery with her loved ones to bid her goodbye. One of our sons-in-law preached her funeral and a more elegant sermon I have never heard. Hearts were lifted because of that message. Larry and I love all our in-laws as if they were our own children. Every one of our three children and their spouses had made a profession of faith in prior years. And each of their lives was a testimony to that.

Now, you have to realize that in our family, no one drank, smoked, or swore...but, for some reason, after Mom "was thrown over," three of her grandchildren got divorces, including the very son-in-law who just a few months before had spoken such beautiful words in front of mom's casket. He just picked up and left his wife and children. What a shock! None of us, including his wife and their children, knew anything was wrong. It was months before we found out that there was another woman. I would have trusted him with my life. I would never have believed that he would have cheated on our daughter. I know that he is saved, but he had a huge fall. As I write this it has been four years since he left. He has since repented but is suffering the consequences of a disobedient life. God always deals with a wayward child of His and sometimes it is very harsh. I only wish the best for him, but our hearts are still and will always be broken over this loss. Rest assured. God will not be mocked. Your sin will find you out.

I can't begin to tell you of the comforting Bible verses that God gave to our daughter in the midst of the blackness that she suffered from her husband's betrayal. She has learned to follow God's path day by day. The hurt that I have seen her endure has been heartbreaking, and the pain that their dad has caused his children has been unbearable for me to watch, but *God is good* and each of the children have grown spiritually in Him.

By this time, I was starting to get used to things going awry. I've lost people and things that were very precious to me. God's surgery knife keeps skillfully cutting and as it does, He's pulled me closer to Him, ever so gently. With each loss, I ran to His cross for comfort. Psalms 147:3 "He healeth the broken in heart and bindeth their wounds." Each time I've called out to Him, I am never turned away. *He is always there* to comfort me with a peace that passeth all understanding.

Lion's Den Library

Not long after Mom's death, I came down with mononucleosis and viral hepatitis. I think the stress got to me and just took me down. I figured reading might help me to recuperate, so down to the local library I trotted to browse over some books. While there, I needed to use the little girl's room, so I traipsed down the hall towards said room. One side of the hall was lined with shelves of newly-released books, which I always have to check. About three feet from the floor, on the shelf, a book caught my eye. Just the right height for a child to see it. Head on! On the front cover was a color picture of a nude couple in a sexual act. I was flabbergasted! I removed the book and took it to the front desk. I did not open it. The jacket was more than I wanted to see! We are hard-pressed in America to mention the name of God, but to have this book where a child can reach it was absolutely ridiculous.

While at the desk, I made a written complaint and made an appointment to speak with the library director the next morning. I decided to check the book out. It would give me more time to figure out my next course of action. I brought the book home and laid it on the counter, still not opening it. It lay there two days before I decided that before I knew what I was objecting to, I had to see what was in it. Inside, on each page, was a full 8x10 color, glossy picture of a completely nude couple in full sexual positions. No holds barred. If a child had gotten his or her hands on it, he would have been scarred for life!

The first thing I did was pray. I paced back and forth on the hardwood in my sock feet until it was polished slick. Finally, I stopped in mid-stride and looked up to Heaven and declared out loud," Yes, Lord, I will do this for you." I knew that this was an issue that needed to be addressed. Publicly.

The next day I met with the director and asked him to please place the book in a place away from young eyes. He refused. The bell had rung!

I promptly sat down and wrote a letter to our small town paper. A couple of days later, I had TV stations calling me, some even knocking at my door. They had read the article that I had supposedly written in the paper. When I finally got the chance to read it, the reporter had reworded it to where it was unrecognizable to me. I was furious. I looked dreadful and felt worse! I was ill and just getting over the loss of Mom, stressed to the gills, when I agreed to meet the reporters at the library.

The library director, who was responsible for the purchase of the book, was caught off guard by the news reporters as was I. This was the same guy who had just a month before, set up a display in the foyer of the library featuring the "gay lifestyle." I am not censoring. We can read what we wish, but, please, protect our young ones. Of course, the news media made the brouhaha about censorship, rather than the protection of children. Since those interviews, I do not, I will not, trust anything that is reported on TV.

I guess the internet lit up with nasty, mean, and degrading comments, both to him and me. I chose not to read them. I started to have panic attacks at night and I really thought that I had forgotten how to sleep! It was terrible! I saw what was done to Sarah Palin, and all I could think was, "Move over, Sarah!" I got a few letters in the mail that I did read. Mostly encouraging ones, but one really malicious one with no name and from a different state. May I say to that person, "You coward!"

I called a meeting with the library committee, but in the meantime, had discussed the matter with a few godly men. Each of them gave me the counsel to step out of it and they would take over. I wanted to come out swinging, but I adhered to their advice and stayed home. The library was swarming with reporters and T.V. crews, but to their chagrin, the prime target made no appearance and everything was kept to a low roar. To sum up this story, the book disappeared and the director "resigned" after seventeen years at our "Lions' Den Library" and moved to Wyoming. You poor people! Watch your children! A year after he moved, I received a phone call from a lawyer in Wyoming. He wanted a first-hand story of the whole incident. The attorney was representing a lady who was suing the same library director over somewhat the same thing that had happened to me. I wish her the best. A footnote: the reporter who unethically changed my wording in my letter to the newspaper was a good friend of the director. Two of a kind, these two.

I always want to have the mindset to say, "Yes, Lord, I will do it for you." Little did I know that I would be saying the same thing to my Father over and over again. Going through the library incident was one of the hardest things that I have ever had to do. I felt alone and unfairly criticized. I had never been picked on in my life! But, oh, I learned so much. I am much tougher now! I could go through that situation standing on my head! "Come on Mr. Director, put up your dukes!"

Another Change

My husband, Larry, was diagnosed with Non-Hodgkin's lymphoma seventeen years ago and has done very well, and still is, but our beautiful property was getting to be more work than he could handle by himself. Trees periodically fell into the creek in the ravine and had to be cut with a chainsaw and moved down steam to keep the waterway open. Each year, it got to be more and more taxing for him and the task of keeping things spotless in our huge home was becoming more and more unappealing to me. After much prayer, we decided to sell. This was the fourth home that we'd had built for us and personally, my favorite piece of land. Our last time was in a wildlife preserve and was hard to leave after ten years, but this one was close to our children and we had been there for twelve years. It was more of a showcase than a home. But no one ever came! Perhaps it was time to downsize. What would we do with all of our furniture? We had five sofa and loveseat sets. One sofa in our bedroom and gobs of fancy things for show and tell. Plus, all kinds of antiques, mostly primitives, in the lower level. I do not call it a basement because it was all windows and doors and finished from top to bottom the same as the rest of the house. I knew every piece of wood and tile that went into that home. We got pretty good with blueprints after building that many times. It was fun for us, like a hobby. We never moved any further than one county away and then ended moving back!

We sold our home quickly, and the task of getting everything distributed, given away, or moved was daunting. We had to be out the day we signed, which in itself was stressful. To clean that size of a home to like-new condition while getting a rental procured was maddening. We got it done and were out by July 4th. I took the move very hard. I didn't want to leave all my little wild animals. Another loss, but at least I had some say in this one.

We moved into a new neighborhood for a year to give ourselves time to decide whether we wanted to build again or to buy an existing house. I have never lived around neighbors. My friends have always been little critters. It was a novelty at first. I walked the "hood" each evening and acquainted myself with numerous folks along the route. A home went up for sale close to where we were renting. Absolutely darling, 2,300 square feet. A lot less space than we were used to having and the lot was tiny compared to our acreage, but we bit the bullet and bought it. Another move. More change in my life. By this time, I was feeling like a man without a country. Nothing seemed the same. Nothing was the same! Nothing but my God! He was still wielding His scalpel.

I tried to squeeze all my annual checkups in between packing boxes. I was never lax with these. Teeth cleaned, eyes checked, blood drawn, and finally the mammogram. Everything checked out fine, as usual. By doing this once or twice a year, things don't get too far out of hand. Always glad to complete each test and go on with my life. But this year would be different. While packing one of the moving boxes, I got a call from my doctor, who informed me that my mammogram had come back abnormal. I was to be at his office the next day.

I didn't worry about cancer. After all, I had a mammogram last year, everything was fine. We had no cancer in the family, that was until a couple of years before, when my younger sister was diagnosed with an aggressive cancer in her left breast. It was a tiny spot and was caught very, very early. She was advised to have a lumpectomy. It was for sure that she would do radiation, but chemo was an option, which she chose to do. Ten days after her first treatment, she started to lose her hair. She took it better than I! I protested when she made me see her without her wig. I was thankful that I wasn't the one who was bald. The thought of losing my hair was horrifying.

I figured if worse came to worse, and I did have cancer, I would do radiation and skip the chemo. That way I would not be hairless. I had one biopsy before and it was benign. I would sail right through this one, also!

I had two places in my right breast. One at the top and one at the bottom. I was diagnosed with Stage 1, grade 3, aggressive cancer. No chance of a lumpectomy. After some further testing, surgery was scheduled for November 8th, 2016. Election day. We had voted a couple of weeks before, so we were good there. I was glad to get October over before my trip to the hospital. October 2nd was our 50th wedding anniversary and we'd had four of our six grandchildren and our oldest son's birthday in that beautiful fall month.

The Holy Spirit seem to be especially close to me the months before surgery and all the way through a years worth of chemo. A couple of months before I was diagnosed, I led a friend's two children to the Lord. I have a friend that I prayed for four years. When I told him about my cancer, he was willing to listen to me again, and then bowed his head and heart to ask forgiveness for his sins and accepted Christ as his savior. I can't tell you how thrilled I was! The next week, the first time I ever met this mechanic who was going to work on our granddaughter's car, bowed his head and heart to God also. What was going on? It seemed like everywhere I went and everyone with whom I spoke, wanted to receive the Lord Jesus as their savior.

I didn't think twice about cancer. I wasn't scared, not even nervous. I was a trooper, met with the surgeon, and ask him to pray with me. I was going to pray but he offered to, instead. I felt that this man had a connection with God. I felt safe. I was to

have removal and reconstruction in the same surgery. Having a breast removed was scary but that
was the price that I had to pay for survival. It still
wasn't as scary to me as losing my mane. One more
thing was gone. Again, my life was forever changed.
Chemo was scheduled on January 5, the day after
my birthday. Losing one's hair may be no big deal
to some, but to me it was right up there after Mom's
and Dad's death. Always making sure that no one
ever saw me without my hair took some innova-
tive and imaginative thinking, but I succeeded! I'm
just now to the point that I will go without a hat
or wig—and then there's the matter of gray hair. I
have never seen myself other than a brunette. Quite
shocking, but it has been a key to opening the con-
versation of cancer and then onto eternity. It has
been amazing how many times I have got to witness to others because of my hair—or lack of it!

The Lord was good in allowing me to heal quickly
from my surgery. The doctor was able to take the
tubes out after one week. So on with the chemo.
twelve weeks of Taxol, which is a very harsh chemo,
and one year of Herceptin which I am still on. But
this is the weird part...just about every week that I
was taking the Taxol, I had the wonderful privilege
of leading someone to Christ. Including oncologists,
nurses, survival guides, one veterinarian, (not for
me! My cat!) The girl who gave me my flu shot at a
pharmacy. It was just strange to see all these people
asking the Lord to forgive them and asking to be
His child. And several others. I know that the fields

are white unto harvest and the laborers are few, but I never knew that it could happen like this. It was like God was making sure my path and those that He had called, crossed. I am humbled each and every time that I have the privilege to witness to a person . The Lord has given me the opportunity to share His love with many, many people this last year and many of them have been saved through His grace. He has used his merciful scalpel on me as needed. I'm sure I am not where I am supposed to be yet, but, He will get me there. I will keep saying, "Yes, Lord, I will do it. It is my privilege. It is my reasonable service."

Am I happy that I have cancer? No! But I am thankful. Yes! Yes! Yes! Thankful to the Lord for this amazing time in my life. Thankful for all the cards and well wishes and for the prayers, lots and lots of prayers. They made my journey easy and light. I have heard people say that they have felt the power of prayer. I can truly tell you that there is such a thing. Each time I went through a chemo treatment I knew that my friends and people that I have never met, were praying for me. I could feel it. I could really feel it!

As I look back, I realize that I have always been full of myself. God had to cut that out too, but I gladly relinquished it. I'm just plain ole me. I want no glory. I want no praise. I only want what God gives me. I write these words of encouragement to the born again believer to get out there and tell of God's salvation. People want to hear and they are eager to listen. I approached a Muslim and told her about Christ's love for her. She did not accept Christ, but she did listen. I spoke with a Wiccan. Again, she didn't accept but she listened. It is not our business whether or not they believe, it is only our duty to tell them. Leave the decisions between them and God. The Holy Spirit will guide. Do not prejudge a person. The least likely person that you think may listen, may be just the one who will be saved. I've had that happen!

The homes that I have had, the jewelry, my health...it is all of no importance compared to Eternity. Through each of these heartbreaking incidences, I have lost something valuable to me. My life has been far from tragic, and I am thankful for that, but, the one thing that I have realized is *the most precious thing*, that gives me more pleasure than anything, is that of winning a soul to Christ. I encourage all born again Christians to please tell others how to be saved. Be bold. Be convincing. And mostly, be sincere. Time is of the essence.

As I write these words , my prayer is that each and every one of you who are saved, will spread the Word, and to each of you who aren't, please humble yourself and ask God to forgive you of all the sins that you have committed and ask the Lord Jesus to be your Savior. I think everyone on God's green earth knows that he is a sinner. We just know. Once we acknowledge that, we must realize that no sin can be in Heaven. There is no way that we can work or buy our way there. It's as simple as asking God to forgive you of your sins and asking the Lord Jesus Christ to come into your heart to be your Lord forever. If you mean that with all of your heart, there is no way that God will not forgive you and accept you as his own.

"Every knee shall bow and every tongue shall confess that Jesus is Lord."

You can do it on Earth while you have the choice, or you can do it at the White Throne Judgement right before you are cast into Hell. Either way, you WILL confess that Jesus Christ is Lord. It's as simple as that. Heaven or Hell? Should it not be obvious?